THE SOUL OF ADULTHOOD

OPENING THE DOORS . . .

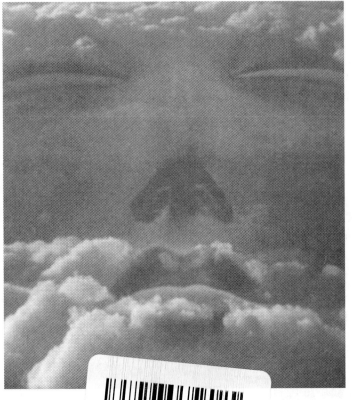

PH.D.

AND LINDA D. FRIEL, M.A.

Friel, John C., (date)
The soul of adulthood: opening the doors—John C. Friel
and Linda Friel.
p. cm
Includes bibliographical references.
ISBN 1-55874-341-3 (trade paper)
1.Adulthood–Psychological aspects. 2. Emotional maturity.
3.Life change events–Psychological aspects. 4. Life cycle,
Human.
I.Friel, Linda D.   II. Title.
BF724.5.F75   1995   95—12560
155.6–dc20   CIP

Publisher: Health Communications, Inc.
              3201 S.W. 15th Street
              Deerfield Beach, Florida 33442-8190

Cover design by Robert Cannata
Photography by: Jim Zuckerman

TO OUR CHILDREN AND YOURS
THAT WE MAY HAVE INTEGRITY ENOUGH
NOT TO FEAR DEATH
SO THAT THEY WILL NOT FEAR LIFE

CONTENTS

PREFACE

Adulthood is a choice. It does not happen because we reach a certain age. Adulthood happens when we choose to pass through the many interconnected doors that lead to the deeper realms of our own souls. The passage of time and the events around us may propel us *toward* adulthood, but we cannot enter into the soul of adulthood until we open these doors and pass through them. Each of the doors to adulthood described herein is opened but briefly, by no means comprehensively. Each chapter is designed to jar loose, pry open, release, prod, prompt and allow connections within the soul of the reader. Each will hopefully lead to deeper reflection and investigation into the doors that have been opened.

As we show in Chapter One, the initial approach to adulthood is often a bumpy one that unleashes a struggle deep inside of the self. As the struggle reaches its conclusion, there is often a process of releasing and grieving, after which the doors slowly open, allowing us to pass through to the next layer of soul. There is a time to struggle and a time to release the struggle, which is why we emphasize these two doors to adulthood throughout this book.

Growing up requires risk, effort and choice, and one of the most important choices is to begin to let go of the extremes in our lives. While living in the extremes is easier at one level, it is terribly painful at another. Facing our disappointments, our loneliness, our narcissism and our victimhood with grace and dignity, and learning healthy entitlement are also key factors in adulthood. Being an adult means being accountable, valuing tradition and discipline, and being able to appreciate the ordinary things in life. And, of course, it also means moving beyond self-esteem myths and painful roles as well as developing our capacity for love, power and graciousness.

Someone who read an earlier version of this manuscript asked an intriguing question: "All of these topics are important for entering adulthood, but if you could only walk through three of these doors, which three would you pick?" The answer came to us fairly easily. We would pick Moving Beyond Extremes, Struggle and Releasing, because with these three capacities well-developed, all of the other doors become accessible.

As you read about these and the other doors to the soul of adulthood in this book, we would like you to remember that these are just a few of the more important ones that we have identified in our own lives and in the lives of those who come to us for help. Above all, remember that adulthood does not happen when we reach a certain age or income level, or when we purchase a certain kind of house or car. Adulthood is a quality of soul that is chosen and earned through the very deepening struggles that life kindly offers us as we progress from birth to death. We can engage these struggles any time right up until the day we die. It is never too late to grow up.

● ● ●

The stories and case studies in this book are based on real people who have graciously permitted us to use their life material after disguising it enough to protect their anonymity.

ACKNOWLEDGMENTS

While the journey into the soul of adulthood never ends, it at least begins with the opening of doors. At times the doors are heavy and we need assistance or guidance, and at times just approaching them is such a scary endeavor that it helps to open them along with others who are on the journey. In that spirit we want to thank all those who have either helped, guided or joined us along the way. We think of you often.

We especially want to thank psychologists James Maddock and Noel Larson, whose intelligence, strength of character and kindness have helped us to become better therapists.

Our deep appreciation goes to Arlene Schmoller for her ability to keep our office afloat while we are out and about trying to open more doors.

Special thanks to our friends and colleagues Mary Pietrini and Gail Wetherell-Sack for their reading of earlier versions of this manuscript and for providing insightful feedback along the way.

Thanks also to Peter Vegso, Gary Seidler and Christine Belleris of Health Communications, Inc., for seeing this project to completion.

Last, but certainly not least, we want to thank Kristin, Rebecca, Scott, Christopher, David, Samuel, Abigail, Bill, Nancy, Brian, Carrie, Rich, John, Mark, Mary, Sandy G., Phyllis, Margo, Larry and Sierra for being in our lives.

Part I

Patterns

Chapter 1

LIFE'S DELICATE STRUCTURES

Life, like a dome of many-colored glass, Stains the white radiance of eternity.

Percy Bysshe Shelley
Adonais, 1821

There are roughly 5.5 billion people on this planet today, and it is most intriguing to realize that we are all nearly identical. It is a simple scientific observation that our genetic, psychological, social, emotional and spiritual similarities far outweigh our differences. The brilliant cross-cultural work of Jerome Kagan on perception, of Jean Piaget on cognitive development and of Erik Erikson on the development of personality shows that humans are human whether we are primitive or industrialized, male or female, African, Asian or Caucasian, tall or short. Scientists now tell us that our genetic makeup is remarkably similar to that of one-celled animals.

The paradox is that each of us also feels so unique that we spend the greater part of our lives trying to explain ourselves to each other in the hope that we can be heard and understood, as if no one else could possibly know what it's like to live inside our skin. We are fascinated with ourselves. Our art, literature, philosophy, psychology, theology, history and science are all about us—descriptions of us, symbolic expressions of us and explanations of us.

If we can agree on nothing else, we seem to agree that one of the primary threads that runs throughout all of human existence is that of struggle. We struggle to live, we struggle with each other over physical and emotional resources, we struggle to avoid pain, to find happiness and to make sense of our lives. And despite all of our seeming uniqueness, there is a form to our internal struggles rivaling the intricacy and beauty of the most complex crystalline structures. These struggles and the structures in which they are embedded are what grace our lives with uniqueness, meaning and depth.

It is our belief that each of us struggles with the same general themes of birth, death, survival, connection and separateness, and that our struggles exist in layers. Where we differ are in the arenas in which we play out our struggles and in the metaphors that we use to symbolize the important elements of our lives. One man struggles much of his life to find a good love while another struggles with a life-threatening illness. One woman struggles to find a cure for cancer while another struggles to resolve the personal horrors of the Holocaust. One struggles in the arena of world politics while another struggles to find peace within the four walls of his own home. Each of us searches for the same things in life, but with metaphorical meaning systems and in arenas that are our very own.

LAYERS OF STRUGGLE

The human soul is layered and faceted with endless manifestations, which is why we are so complex, so fascinating. Struggles exist in layers because our lives, our meaning systems and our very core selves are layered and faceted. Some people look at each other and see only a surface, which is why we are sometimes so shocked by others' behavior. A neighbor commits suicide, a famous person kills a friend, our favorite minister admits to having affairs, and we feel our very foundations shake. When all we respond to is the surface layer of someone, we miss their truth and depth. And while there is no way that we would have the time or energy to look into each human being with the depth of a close friend or lover, if we do not look deeply into ourselves and at least one other person, we miss out on a crucial aspect of life.

Social and political pundits struggle with these layers all the time as they try to simplify life for us in a 90-second television analysis. They might say, "Well, he was obviously a fraud, rotten to the core." But is that all he was? Or does it simply take too much time to say, "He was a fraud in this aspect of his life, he was honorable in that aspect, he was confused in yet another, and perhaps a saint in yet another?" Each human being has multiple layers. A woman may work hard because she likes nice material things, but she may also work hard because she enjoys her work, and deep down inside she may work hard because she truly cares about improving the human race. It is not a contradiction to say that she likes nice things and also cares deeply about humanity, but some people would find this paradox incomprehensible.

Most major theories of human development imply these layers as well. For example, in Erik Erikson's stages of development we don't just have a trust versus mistrust crisis when we are newborns. Questions of trust versus mistrust appear in new forms from then onward, right up until the day we die. Each stage or crisis through which we pass incorporates transformed versions of the ones before it so that by the time we are struggling with intimacy versus isolation in early adulthood we carry along inside of it redefined issues of trust, autonomy, initiative, competence and identity.

Research on adult development tells us that as we move from one era to another in our lives we are challenged to make sense of all that has gone before. When we are 23 and moving out into the world, we look back and realize that something is ending and something else is opening up, producing sadness and exhilaration. As this process begins, we struggle with which parts of the past to embrace, which parts to mourn, which parts to change and which parts to put on hold. With new eyes, more mature eyes, we look back and say, "Oh, I once believed that everything my parents said and did was good, or bad; but now I can sort through it all and see that it isn't that simple. Some of it was good, some not so good and some I can take or leave." Life is so wonderful, because at each crossroad we are offered yet another chance to gather up all the loose threads and baffling paradoxes and make some deeper sense of them. Life becomes a beautiful ongoing mystery filled with new discoveries about old events, all the way along, which is the antithesis of boredom.

A SOULFUL LOVE AFFAIR

We knew a man who had a longstanding love affair, but it wasn't with another person. Anyone who knew of his love and admiration for his wife could have determined that. His secret love affair, known only tangentially to those close to him, was with the place where he grew up. And the memories, images, ghosts, contradictions and longings that haunted him as they tumbled out of his unconscious mind were a seemingly random amalgamation of sights, sounds, tastes and textures from that timeless space within his own soul that had been carefully carved and formed during his childhood. Over the years the place of his youth had taken up residence, had etched itself into his very wholeness, where it served him as an intricate arena for the resolution and integration of deeper and deeper parts of himself as he grew older and matured. His passion for life as he was now living it struggled with his deeper urges to return home in some kind of metaphorical, if not literal way, releasing infinitesimal waves of hope and regret, sadness and joy, disappointment and exhilaration, and pain; and he was sustained and enriched by them, as seen in this more recent journal entry he shared with us.

> *I can finally respect it rather than fear it. For the most part, this struggle rests comfortably, with elegance and grace, in a delicate, nearly invisible corner of my life, its tension balanced tautly like the strings of a violin. When it becomes too tight and complains, it does so with kindness. It is courteous and civilized, knowing when it isn't welcome but willing to share in my life when I am ready. When it feels neglected, it nudges me and asks to be heard. This arena of struggle has so many twists and turns to it that over the years it has developed into a complex ally filled with unexpected messages and meanings for me. On its very surface, on its most concrete, literal, sensory plane, it is made up of my ambivalent feelings about where I would like to live.*

Part of me loves where I am, and part of me longs to move back to the place of my youth.

My more peaceful childhood memories constantly tweak and poke and prod me with hypnotically deep sensory impressions of soft, warm, dry summer air infused with the earthy scent of eucalyptus and bay laurel. As I breathe the memories deeper and deeper into my soul, the smell of the hot, dry powdery earth mixed with manzanita and sage surround me, engulf me, take command of my being. A perfect blue sky fills my consciousness with an almost erotic warmth as I feel the hot, comforting rays of the sun first touch my skin and then pass into my body, where they circulate and gently soothe places of loneliness and fear that reside deep inside me.

A bird sings in the back yard, jarring me out of my sensory trance, and I continue about my daily tasks while another part of me is left to feel and sort through the tiny aftershocks and lingering reverberations of a sadness, or a loss, or a hope, or an anticipation and excitement about what was, what might have been, what is or what could be. I long to go back, and then I am immeasurably grateful that I am already home.

THE SURFACE STRUCTURE

Oftentimes, when we first begin to wrestle with issues of adulthood, the surface of our lives is disrupted and our forays into our arenas of struggle are confused and intense, like a foot soldier charging onto a battlefield with energy and determination but lacking the deeper comprehension of the events at hand. Our metaphors and life images may intrude into our consciousness with the force of an inexperienced burglar breaking a window or a lock, and when we come back to the here and now it might be with a startled jolt, as if we were being yanked out of a sound sleep by a disgruntled parent angry that we were late for school.

And so, as is quite normal, rather than reflecting upon what was contained in his soul, this man spent most of his 20s acting out his struggle by returning home over and over, trying to recapture something on one visit, trying to undo something on another, but always being in motion enough that the clatter drowned out the faint voices coming from the next layer down inside of himself. The deeper meanings and exquisite intricacies of life came in crude bursts and fits, evaporating quickly, leaving no trail, no evidence of having been there. But then in his late twenties he had kneaded and worked the surface of his struggle enough that something began to change.

Something has been happening inside of me. The first sign came to me as I jogged through my old neighborhood. As I turned the corner and came upon the little house nestled among hedges and old shade trees and bathed in late morning sunlight, I felt a timeless, disconnected, painful emptiness fill my chest and radiate into my stomach; and as the last faint traces of it receded back into my depths, something inside of me took note that this was a moment of historical significance. Since returning home from this vacation I am noticing many negative feelings bubbling up to the surface and creeping into my conversations. I speak with regret and disdain for how my home town has changed in recent years and of how blind I have been to its many shortcomings when I was a child growing up there. The natural beauty of the area is terribly overrated by the natives and the people are as shallow and as lost as some say, I tell myself. I wonder how I could have been so unaware all of these years.

At about the same time he began to experience intense disruptions in his work and relationships. Painful memories were extruded from deep inside of him, bursting forth with a blinding fury that wrenched his foundation from beneath him. He cried, he was angry, he felt despair and confusion, he went in and out of painful relationships, he denied that anything was wrong and then he crashed into the depths once more. Down and down he fell, spiraling through a maelstrom of torment, fear and loneliness. His dreams and memories were no longer warm and soothing as they had once been. Ghosts and memories of pain held sway. The enveloping magic of night that he once experienced became a time of lonely darkness.

From somewhere inside, a sharp flash shattered the calm with an image of a little child laying in his bed, listening to fighting, adults out of control, home no longer safe. The fear he had carefully tucked away for so many years reared up from the depths and began to strangle him. He screamed in terror, silently, alone, inside of his soul. And then from an even deeper place within him, hidden far away for safety and protection, another part of the struggle raised up briefly, told him that he would endure, and then returned to its place of safety. Gradually, he could see that his life was deepening and that his pain was beginning to subside. The emotional storms were shorter and less intense. He was now ready to move through another layer of self and to open one of the doors to adulthood.

GRIEVING

As we move from one stage of our lives to another, we also move into the next deeper layer of our souls. It is a painful time, a time of confusion and searching. But it is also an exciting time filled with the promise of better things to come, a time of consolidation, integration and understanding. We let go of one part of our meaning system and open up to a new part.

One day I became aware that both parts of the struggle had finally been revealed to me, and I knew I was ready for the hard part. I was scared, and on my next visit to my birthplace, my ambivalence was palpable, and I was awash in sadness and a pervasive unease. The furious battle on the surface was nearing its conclusion and the deeper, more peaceful struggle beneath was preparing to emerge. I grieved the loss that was upon me, the loss of childhood hopes and dreams, of the textures and sights and sounds and fragrances that had entranced me and sustained me these many years.

I watched the fog creep over the crests and down the sides of the coastal mountains, and it felt ominous, cold and lonely, instead of comforting, soothing and mystical as it often had been in the past. I looked out at the glorious sun sinking into the ocean at day's end and felt my spirit fade into a dark, hopeless void. The damp, cool forest, permeated with the musky smell of redwood bark and ferns, threatened to pull me into a tangled underworld of despair and emptiness. I struggled gallantly with a deep loneliness as my dignity began to push its way up from the rich, dark earth beneath my feet.

Lunch with an old friend warmed my spirit for a brief moment, connecting me with the roots that brought life to my soul. Time with my dying parents heightened the struggle. Their lives were flickering, running out, and I resisted accepting them for who they were. Part of me hoped that they would become something more that I still needed. I saw two old people who were argumentative, childish and unhappy. I felt disappointed and betrayed as the sadness kept seeping through the cracks in the layers of my unconscious. Outside, the fog flowed effortlessly into the bay around cliffs and rocks, beneath bridges, along roadways, between piers and pilings, insinuating itself into my life without resistance, leaving no damage, no pain, no scars, until it was embedded in the physical world around me with as much permanence as the buildings and tunnels and highways now enshrouded in mist.

A Christmas Day cracked into consciousness, shocking and jarring the dreamy, disconnected emptiness with a vivid memory of a cold, rainy winter day, new bicycles, wrappings and bows strewn about the floor, pretend giggles and laughter from a child who was confused, lonely, and spent from the intensity of a holiday celebration punctuated by extremes of fantasy and unacknowledged family pain. If only someone had asked, "Are you okay?"

The fog slowly released its grip from the cracks and crevices, cypress and redwoods, harbors and inlets, making its unpredictable decision to return to its home far out at sea. To me, the fog is a soothing mystery, an omen, a symbol, a comforting universal presence, like the spirit. Fog comes and goes in endless rhythms, with limitless variations. Sometimes it creeps in slowly with thin, blind fingers *that search for entrances and openings under a magical moonlit sky, carefully lingering low atop the water for a day or so and then receding just as unobtrusively as it had come. The next time it might roar in from the ocean, riding cold, gusty winds high over the mountaintops, pushing deep across the bay, blocking the sun and sky with boldness and strength. The cooling, soothing fog is there to enclose all things in a shroud of reflection, to tie up loose ends, to connect all things that exist separately during the clear light of day, to heal.*

RELEASING AND DEEPENING

The next day, the early morning sunlight sparkled and danced on the needles of the tall sugar pines outside the window as the sun blazed on the horizon. The man's retina worked furiously to send the signals of warmth and awakening to his cerebral cortex while the deeper recesses of his soul struggled to receive the message being sent. The last trails of mist from the previous day along with the exquisitely reconnected ghosts and images from his past gave the sunlight a dry, grassy hillside on which to play. He walked outside and let the sun warm him as a bright blue sky opened up above the quiet mountains and vast expanse of sea. The door was now open.

When I talked gently with my parents today, I saw two people who had managed their lives with brilliance and courage, taking risks, making vows and struggling gallantly to live and die with meaning and purpose. My heart went out to them. My history was connected to their history, my pain and fears were connected to theirs, my depth had come from the generations of those who went before me with all of their wisdom and ignorance, bitterness and disease, sorrow and ecstasy. And these two old people, their bodies weak and their minds beginning to fog, were the last of those previous generations. As I struggled with these contradictions, something deep within me began to open, and then it was time for me to return home.

The edges of this tiny opening gratefully and willingly began to loosen and crumble in his early 30s as his soul deepened, allowing the surface struggle between him and his childhood pain to slowly dissolve like the skin of a serpent being shed to make room for new growth. As this happened, he was faced with a new form of the struggle, with a new face and new depth.

The question was no longer, "Are you okay?" Now the question was, "Who are you, and what is your part in all of this?" Even more disconcerting and exciting was the gradual awareness that the question could only come from the deeper parts of himself. As he moved toward the inner layers of his soul, he found himself moving into the present more, and for the first time in his life, he was able to make out the faint outlines of self, and to perceive and comprehend the differences between self and self-absorption.

THE PRESENCE OF ANGELS

As we continue to mature throughout adulthood, our struggles find a comfortable residence within our core self, and we are able to appreciate the incredibly complex structures of personality and life that we have constructed over the years. And we can see that even at its most surface layer, during our early 20s and before, the struggles have always been inside of us, far down in our very souls. Where we live, how we choose to structure our lives, our friends and partners, all of these are matters of personal preference. What matters most in terms of life structure and maturity is that we can eventually respond from our own acknowledged depths rather than from the pain of what may have been done to us.

We continue to entertain these inner struggles, and with every passing year, our souls take on more complexity, more shape and definition, more clarity, more wholeness. As the struggle at one level nears completion, we watch with excitement and anxiety as the features of the next layer reveal themselves. The longer this process continues the less disruptive the struggles become, and the more subtle, exquisite and ecstatic they become. For example, one year this man's struggle with where to live revealed to him that he missed his father. He had been so busy with the funeral arrangements and the other details of his life that he hadn't taken the time to honor the good things about his father that he had always appreciated. A few years later, his struggle showed him how hard he had tried all of his life to be responsible and that he needed those close to him to acknowledge it. A few years later still, in one of his more vivid encounters with these ghosts and images and longings from his past, he realized that the fear of scarcity, of not having enough, was pushing him to try to live too much instead of simply being in his life.

Recently, during one of those more open, tumultuous struggles that occasionally visited him, he was given a gift beyond compare. As the layer of the previous struggle began to be sloughed off, he uncovered and began to comprehend faith—the faith that the intensity of our struggles wasn't created to hurt us, but to inform us, and that the confusion takes the form of a tornado at times so that we can feel where we still hurt. It teaches us that struggle is a generous part of life and that the frightening, confusing battles appear only when necessary, only with the intensity that is necessary, and never with the desire to harm. The frightening part of the struggle finally had a place within him to rest.

> *While on a walk one day I was surprised and suddenly overcome with wonder when I thought I spied the little sprites and spirits frolicking in the woods with their dancing faces and soulful eyes, filled with magic and mischief. Perhaps it was only the chickadees singing in the trees or the puppy playing with the pine cones, I laughed to myself. I wasn't too sure. But my soul was filled with mirth. Soon after that I felt the presence of an angel. I was worried about money. Soon after my father died my wife had a dream in which my father appeared to her and told her to let me know that I had all that I needed. She awoke from the dream and shared it with me, and her dream became a part of my soul and a part of my struggle, and it deepened my love for her beyond measure.*

> *I continue to struggle with my fears, but from that day forward I was visited by the ghosts and images and memories and longings of that mysterious morning when she shared the dream with me, and every time I look into her eyes or see her sparkling smile across the room, I shiver and know there are angels. She graces my life, blesses my children, challenges my fears and warms my heart.*

Throughout every day, across every year and within every decade, I have become part of her struggles and she has become part of mine. The depth of her dreams collides with the power of mine. We laugh and cry and yell and love across a universe of dishes and paperwork and children and bills. When our deeper fears ask to be heard at the same time, our struggle materializes into a whirlwind of pain and confusion, filling us with anxiety and doubt. And then one of us feels the presence of an angel, and then the other.

BETWEEN BIRTH AND DEATH

We are born, and we die. In between these two great events we are given a life that is punctuated by struggle, change, joy, heartache, ecstasy, hurt, sadness, loss and exhilaration. The slice of one man's life that you just finished reading is actually very ordinary, although some might not be comfortable with that analysis because of the particular nature of his struggles. Although the arenas and backdrops may be different on the surface, each of us has struggles very much like his. Life is like that. It is a marvelous gift that by its very nature asks each one of us to face challenges of progressive growth and deepening. Yet as each life becomes more complex and full, it also becomes more ordinary, which is one of the wonderful mysteries that is shared by each person who moves through childhood and into adulthood. It is up to us to choose at each step along the way whether or not we are ready and willing to accept these challenges.

Learning to be in life fully, as an adult, is what this book is about. Each of the remaining chapters stands alone and can be read in any order that pleases the reader. Each represents one of the innumerable issues or challenges that greets us as we live in and create our lives; and as we struggle with any one of these issues, we, like the man you just read about, are allowed to experience life with more depth, gratitude and grace. We are allowed to enter the soul of adulthood when we make the conscious choice to pass through each of the doors described in these chapters.

As you continue reading, we invite you to view struggle not as something to be avoided at all cost, but as that which truly sustains and gives meaning to life. We invite you to open your hearts and minds to the challenges and complexities represented by each of these doors, and as you do, we wish you a generous journey of filling your soul.

Part II

The Doors
to Adulthood

Chapter 2

EXTREMES

*Our senses can grasp nothing that is extreme . . .
too far or too near prevents us seeing; too long or
too short is beyond understanding; too much truth
stuns us.*

Blaise Pascal
Pensées, 1670

The soul of adulthood tries to live passionately, with balance and grace; and intensely, with subtlety and understatement. If there are many doors that must be opened in order to embrace the soul of adulthood, then letting go of the extremes is perhaps the master key that unlocks all the rest. This is hard to understand, because we tend to live a life of extremes when we are still controlled by the ghosts of the past. In our struggle to compensate for the shortages that we endured as children, we often mistake extremism for passion, which leads to pathological intensities instead of fullness of living. It is one of the more troubling paradoxes of human beings that the more pain we experience as children, the more of it we will recreate as adults despite our resolute vows not to do as adults what was done to us as children.

A woman has a terribly lonely and exhausting childhood, because her parents require her to carry many more responsibilities than is healthy for a child. To make up for it, she ensures that her own children never have to do any chores at all, preferring that they enjoy childhood so fully that her own emotional shortages might be magically filled through her children. But the net result is that she feels tired and lonely much of the time because she is doing everything for everyone else; and she feels used and unloved because no one helps her with all of her work, just like it was when she was growing up.

The other sad result of this well-intentioned strategy is that her children will also grow up to experience life in the extremes, because they have lived extremely as children. Children who never have any responsibilities while growing up become adults who are constantly disappointed by how much effort it takes to live, frustrated by how many boring details there are in each day, and befuddled when others view them as spoiled, demanding or unrealistic in their expectations. The end result of living in this extreme is that the young adult feels isolated, lonely and ultimately exhausted by the simple tasks of life that others accept gracefully.

Passionate, balanced living is one of the most important aspects of soulful adulthood; and it is quite different than a life of boredom and mediocrity. This is especially true of our most cherished relationships. Many people who have not yet moved to the deeper layers of their life-struggle believe that balanced relationships will lack intensity and power, and that they will eventually become boring and lifeless unless we push them to the outer edges all the time. In fact, while relationships that exist on these outer edges of intensity may feel as if they are filled with life, they are actually shallow, empty and devoid of much meaning other than crisis. True passion is not pathologically intense. It is deep, mysterious, gracious, tactful, filled with life and neither boring nor terrifying.

As we gradually move from childhood into adulthood, we begin to discern and appreciate the subtleties of life; and our minds expand enough for us to comprehend the limitations of rigid, simplistic thinking. We can then begin a successful struggle to let go of damaging extremes.

DEPENDENCY EXTREMES

One of the most common of these struggles surrounds our efforts to create balance in our dependencies. A man came to us complaining about his partner whom he described as so dependent and clingy that he feared that he would be completely absorbed by her. His fear of being absorbed and assimilated by her was so intense that he had done everything except formally dissolve the relationship. When he traveled for business she became intensely controlling and jealous, worrying that he would meet someone else and leave her. When he was tired from a particularly hard day at work, she couldn't bear to give him a half-hour of solitude before he settled in with her for the evening. No matter where he went she always had to go with him, and she pursued him sexually with a hunger that he described as coming from a bottomless pit of need.

It would be easy to sympathize with this man and get angry along with him for the pain that his partner was causing him, but there is always more to relationships than first meets the eye. We asked him why he had been drawn to her in the beginning, and he was taken aback momentarily before he answered that he had most liked her gentleness and femininity, and that he had been warmed and flattered by her admiration of his strength and independence. As we carefully helped this man redirect his focus from her to himself, he gradually became aware of how he had naively simplified the problem. In so doing, he opened the door to the next layer of self, which permitted him to come face to face with his own deep neediness. At first he was ashamed and angry at the possibility that he, too, was dependent. His surface logic told him that he was the most independent person he knew, because he traveled alone, enjoyed the challenges of meeting new people and seeing new places, and because he never felt sad, hurt or vulnerable. But his true self deep inside told him that he had simply denied his dependencies altogether, leaving him lonely, isolated and longing for a kind of real closeness that he had never experienced.

Then one day he wept openly during a session and said that he had been hiding his dependency for so many years because he was afraid that he would either be rejected or absorbed by the people close to him. Predictably, as he became more vulnerable his partner at first tried to absorb him by feeding on this opening in his outer shell, and he grew even more frightened and angry, disappointed that all of his hard work was in vain. He realized that she had been waiting for this opening for many years and was starved for an emotional connection with him, which set the stage for both of them to let go of the extremes.

Over the succeeding months we worked with them as a couple, and as they each acknowledged the mutually destructive dependencies that they had brought into the relationship at the beginning, they were able to slowly move away from their extreme positions. They fought and struggled in the beginning. He wanted instant results and so did she. But the more they worked with it, the more they were able to grasp the difference between closeness and smothering on the one hand, and between independence and isolation on the other. After several months had passed they came to their session and announced that they had fallen in love with each other. They announced that they still struggled with clinging and isolation now and then, but they were also having more and more periods of deep connection. They were especially excited and amazed to tell us that they had begun to feel passionate about all sorts of ordinary things in their lives.

BELIEF EXTREMES

Living in the extremes is usually a reminder to us that at our core we are still living in fear, which is surely evident in the case of extreme belief systems. A man batters his wife and justifies it by saying that she didn't get his permission before going out to dinner with her friends. He may even quote the Bible, saying that the man is the head of the household and a wife should be subservient to her husband. He may be a Biblical scholar with the ability to debate scripture for days at a time. Regardless of his rationale for the abuse, it is clear that the typical batterer does so because he is terrified that if he gives up some of his control he might lose his wife.

The extremes of ethnic and racial prejudice are rooted in the primitive biological wiring that tells us to be wary of the unknown, a mechanism that is very important for our individual survival. When such fears are balanced they do serve us well, as in the case of a stranger at our hotel room door who claims to be from the maintenance department. If we live with the childish belief that all people are trustworthy, we might put our lives at risk; and if we have the damaged child's belief that no one can be trusted, we might suffer with an air conditioner or toilet that doesn't work properly. If we are balanced in our beliefs about the safety of other human beings, we might keep the door locked until we call the front desk to see if it is a legitimate repair visit and then ask the man if he has an identification card.

Someone who has embraced the soul of adulthood can look at the world and say, "Some Caucasian, African or Middle Eastern people on this planet are decent, kind and trustworthy, and some are not." A person who is stuck in the pain of childhood terror will need to simplify the world much more because she feels so overwhelmed. Her outer logic will find much comfort when she can say, "All Caucasians, or all men, or all Catholics cannot be trusted—they are all bad." While her outer logic feeds on these statements, her inner self will be screaming, begging her to let go of the extremes so that her terror can be soothed by the warmth of human intimacy.

In our work with people in pain, struggles with extreme beliefs come in many shapes and sizes. Wounded men say that all women are out to get them. Frightened people might misinterpret their Christianity to support a belief that all Muslims are evil. A woman afraid of her reasonable anger does everything in her power to be nice under all circumstances, believing that if she ever shows her anger she will be deemed a bad person or will be abandoned. Each of us carries a set of beliefs about the world, and those beliefs are like the software instructions stored in a computer. We don't have to think about them very much, because they just run autonomously, until something goes wrong, and then we become painfully aware of them.

If we grew up in a rigid, autocratic family, we may unconsciously form the extreme belief that all authority is bad or that all rules are bad; or we may believe that authoritarianism is the only way to live. Once these beliefs are loaded onto our unconscious hard drive, they run automatically, serving us well until a malfunction occurs. It might come when we admit that we have been fired from five successive jobs because we start unnecessary fights with our superiors; or when our children become truant and destructive in school because we have chosen to raise them without rules and limits, or because we have been severely restrictive with them.

If I believe that as a good friend I must always be there for you regardless of the circumstances, I may find myself in relationships with people who drain me until I am near exhaustion. If I believe that I should be able to handle all of my problems by myself, I will surely encounter problems that can't be solved as a result of that belief, for the simple reason that no person can do it all. What is worse is that I will be very trapped and alone in the world, because I will never let anyone see my vulnerable side.

RELEASING EXTREMES

The extremes in which we become mired are as numerous and varied as the people on earth. As we help people move into adulthood, we look at emotional extremes around dependency, anger, fear, shame, hurt, sadness, guilt, loneliness and even happiness. We also examine extremes of belief around issues of structure and limits, trust, sexuality, religion, friendship, abandonment, control, power and many others. Lastly, we help our clients evaluate the extremes in their behavior, because unless our actions change, we may feel like adults and believe that we are adults but we won't be adults. And so we look at behavioral extremes such as working too much or hardly working at all, never exercising or being driven to exercise all the time, taking dangerous risks or never doing anything remotely exciting, and arguing all the time or never standing up for one's opinion, to name a few.

In every instance, when a person looks into the face of the extremes in which he is living, the first reaction is to defend against it. We might say, "I'm not rigid, I just think children need to have lots of structure," or, "People aren't trustworthy anymore—times have changed." As we allow the outer layer of logic to be challenged by the life around us, we become scared because our true self knows that to live with balance and passion takes risk. It is at this moment that the connection between life and death is illuminated, because to leap into the unknown is what living and dying well are all about. When a man begins to release his extreme dependency on his partner it is as if a part of him is dying. He says, "If I move away from my partner, a little bit so that more of me can grow, I might be abandoned, and if I am abandoned, I might not live." A woman who releases her extreme independence as she begins to move toward intimacy says, "If I move closer, and if I put down my shield, I might be absorbed by the other."

It is less confusing at our outer layers when we live in an all-or-none world. If we believe that all religious leaders are bad or good, then we don't have to think or make choices, we can simply dislike or like all religious leaders. But deep inside there is a part of us that knows life isn't that simple, and so at that level we are in agony. It is much like spending most of our life in prison where, although we may feel mean, angry and powerful or passive, defeated and helpless, we eventually become so accustomed to prison life that the thought of doing anything else is actually more disturbing than prison itself.

And so as we make the leap away from the extremes, down into our deeper self, and struggle with the ambiguity that ensues, we discover that life is much more than black-and-white. Suddenly, a whole world of complexity and richness opens up before us—a world filled with light and dark, tints and hues, tastes and smells, sights, sounds, textures and subtle intensities we never imagined existed. We can see the evil in the world, the wondrous good, and also the vast, perplexing fields of life in between.

The paradox, of course, is that as we allow the ambiguities of life to find a comfortable resting place deep inside of us, we find that life becomes much easier to understand and accept. Life *is* complicated, but if we can accept that fact it becomes much easier to live it. That is why we speculate that the master key that unlocks the other doors to the soul of adulthood is this one.

Chapter 3

STRUGGLE

Life is a romantic business. It is painting a picture, not doing a sum—but you have to make the romance. And it will come to the question how much fire you have in your belly.

Oliver Wendell Holmes, 1911

LIFE'S CANVAS

We can only experience life through struggle. It provides the canvas for our life's paintings. Without it we would have brushes and paints, but no artwork, no place for our creation to exist. Struggle provides the background and the arena in which life is played out and lived. Even in our dreams we struggle to make sense out of what is inside and outside of us, sometimes gently and hypnotically, sometimes fitfully or frighteningly.

The renewed enthusiasm about the brilliant work of Carl Jung indicates how much we long to acknowledge the importance of struggle within our souls, and how we hunger for metaphors and symbols that can give a clear voice to the complexity within us and around us. Jung actually encouraged his clients to paint or draw their dreams on paper or canvas, and he noted that ". . . it is one thing for a person to have an interesting conversation with his doctor twice a week . . . and quite another thing to struggle for hours at a time with refractory brush and colours . . ."

From the moment we are born, we are meant to engage life, to grapple with it, to be molded by it and to mold it, to understand its complexities and its seeming unreasonableness, to realize all of our potentialities, and to survive. Many people today are interested in spirituality, believing that the spiritual world is something mystical and unknowable, and that to understand the spirit we must try to live in a world beyond that of our five senses. But spirituality begins at birth when we express our will to live. From this barely formed seed of creation that is a new life, we gradually expand our will, our spiritedness, out into the larger world beyond us, until somewhere in adulthood we catch a glimpse of energy and life that is deeper than simply the will to survive. It is then that we are able to begin to comprehend spirituality in its deeper forms. But it all begins with, and continues to include, the will to live.

Many of us try hard to remove the struggle from our lives, as if struggle were a bad thing. We take pills, drink alcohol, watch television endlessly or practice our religions compulsively, without soul, in the hopes of reducing the discomfort generated by our many struggles. We believe that we are improving our lives by doing these things, but the irony is that without struggle we wouldn't be able to experience life at all. We would be dead. Even in a coma we are struggling primitively, unconsciously, biologically.

THE GOSSAMER VEIL

A woman we know had been engaged in a longstanding struggle with ambivalence. While her dynamic career paid extremely well and provided much travel and interesting challenges, part of her wrestled with a deep longing for permanence and stability. The energy from this ambivalence had created marvelous complexity, facets, structures, accommodations and an architecture to her external life rivaling the Cathedral of Notre Dame. The very external structures she had created to house her ambivalence were reflections and manifestations of the deeper realms of her inner self that were longing to express themselves. Deep in her soul there resided a part of her that struggled with questions of life, death, meaning, abandonment and love.

The external architecture of her life included two homes in two different cities with two very different climates, and two lovers, one who was quiet, down-to-earth and rooted in a fairly predictable daily life; and another who was dynamic, exciting, worldly and somewhat unpredictable. They were kind, honorable men and both of them had potential for a long-term relationship with a woman. At times she dreamt of an exciting life filled with adventure and drama, and then her feelings shifted quickly, filling her with a hunger for home, children and predictability. Her magical ability to hold these two urges in a fantastically balanced tension along the outskirts of danger and boredom allowed a gossamer veil of poignancy to cover every surface, edge and corner of her existence. When the breath of a warm summer breeze touched the loose edges of this veil, she would feel a sensuousness inside of her that was almost too fragile to bear.

One day she awoke to find that her unconscious mind had been hard at work for many of the preceding months. She had a dream in which she lived in a villa in the hills of Tuscany, and it was a bright, warm summer morning. She was in bed and the room was getting uncomfortably warm as the day opened up before her sleeping body; she dreamt that she was struggling very hard to find a place of cool respite from the heat of a conflict that was not clear to her. In the dream, the large wooden shutters, over 100 years old, gently yielded to a cool, soft breeze that had been pushing its way into the bed chamber from the valley below. The breeze caressed her febrile brow and carried off the heat of the struggle, and then she awoke. She looked at the sheer white curtains dancing in the cool morning breeze coming off the lake on which her home was built, and she realized that, indeed, the shutters had opened up that morning, perhaps at the request of the breath inside of her that was there to work magic and unravel mysteries.

A few months after having the dream, this woman became aware of something opening deep inside of her. Somewhere near the center of her soul she felt a veil rise up, carried aloft by some gentle force, and then something released. Soon after that she was able to choose the man and the lifestyle that she truly desired. Her struggle became less intense and more subtle as her spirit went deeper inward and farther into the larger world outside of her, and she felt peace. As she looked back at the fifteen years between 22 and 37, she realized that without the struggle she would not have seen as much of the world, she would not have felt as many different sunsets, she would not have built as complex a life and she would not have had as much to surrender when it was time to do so. She was filled with gratitude then, knowing that not every person has the gifts or the good fortune to live the life that she had been able to live during those years. Cool breezes carry healing messages of sorrow and joy, but only if we are open to them, and only if we are willing to wait.

THE SAINT AND THE BOTTLE

A brilliant, dear friend of ours who died in his late 60s just a few years ago struggled with alcoholism his entire adult life. Barely in his 20s, he spent his sizable inheritance and then jumped from one career to the next, losing each job because of his drinking. He participated in chemical dependency treatment seven times over many years. He had one period of sobriety for seven long years before drinking again. A few years later he fell in love and was given the choice to sober up or leave the relationship. He entered treatment as a patient for the last time, and remained sober for many years, right through to the day he died.

It would be easy to look back at his long life and quickly surmise that much of it was wasted, and we would be partially correct in our assessment. Or we could choose to look back with care and depth, and see that this man's life was filled with a richness and complexity beyond compare. He touched so many souls with his laughter, genius and stubbornness. Tales of his outrageous alcohol-induced death-defying antics filled AA meetings with uncontrollable belly-laughter in church basements across America. He was warmhearted, rigid and filled from top to bottom with simple love. During his bouts with alcohol, scores of people looked at what was happening to him and chose to quit drinking as a result of what they saw. And during his years of sobriety, he impacted literally hundreds of people as he became one of the most competent and effective alcoholism counselors we have ever met.

He had such spirit, and his soul had such complexity in the unique patterns of light and dark that it had woven as he lived out his enormously tormented, magnificently blessed days of alcoholism and sobriety. It is hard to imagine who he might have been or what he might have done had he not been an alcoholic, but we are certain that he would be the first to assert that his struggle with alcoholism brought him the greatest dignity, peace of mind and depth of soul imaginable. He came from a wealthy family, was educated in the finest schools, squandered a large fortune, nearly drank himself to death many times, hardly ever made much money once he sobered up, and yet we say he had great dignity and peace. When a Betty Ford, Peter O'Toole or Mickey Mantle goes into recovery for alcoholism, many of us find it easier to see the value of the struggle, because public figures like that often manage to hang onto their wealth and fame. We like to think that our struggles will always have financially successful endings, too. But successful struggles are best measured in units of inner peace rather than in dollars.

THE DEEP ROOTS OF STRUGGLE

We are born with a deeply rooted biological longing that remains with us until the moment we die. We grasp, root, suck, attempt to get away from pain and cry reflexively, without conscious intention, in order to get our needs met so that we can endure. We are biologically programmed to struggle for food, water, comfort and care, so that when these things are not provided, we protest most loudly until they are. And fortunately for us, we don't always immediately get what we want.

As Sigmund Freud grappled with his complex theories of human psychology, he came to believe that it is only through frustration and struggle that we are able to develop an ego, which in his model is the part of us that handles the practical realities of everyday life. While the id houses our primitive unconscious urges and provides the drive and energy for action and growth, and is responsible for our dreams, fantasy and creativity, it is the ego that actually gets things done. Without an ego we would fantasize and long for what we want and need, but we would never do anything to get them. We wouldn't even know where to begin.

A newborn is totally undifferentiated and completely egocentric, unable to tell the difference between himself and others. When he nurses at his mother's breast, her breast becomes a part of him. His primitive self cannot separate his own desires and fantasies from the existence of others. When the baby is hungry, he fantasizes being fed and seemingly from nowhere a breast appears, leaving him with a remarkably unrealistic sense of his own power. So it is good when one day his mother is momentarily busy and a breast does not appear right away, because the ensuing frustration challenges the baby to question the limits of fantasy and helps him to begin the separation from his narcissism, so that he can gradually comprehend both the "me" and the "not-me." This gentle, consistent frustration of a baby's needs in a way that is not over-whelming allows the baby to develop and grow up.

When an adult expects his fantasies to materialize out of thin air without struggle, he is said to be immature and narcissistic. He will have great difficulty maintaining separation in his relationships, at times actually confusing his own feelings with those of others, and he will require almost constant attention and admiration even though he may pronounce loudly how self-reliant he is. He will be an infant in adult's clothing, and will thus be miserable inside of himself and to those around him.

The solution to the question of how much frustration is healthy lies in the hidden realms of the extremes. Wise parents understand its helpfulness in small, regular doses, most of which are metered out by the vagaries of life itself. But other parents get lost in their own childhood shortages and then either deprive their children in the hopes of making them strong, or give their children everything without struggle in the hopes that their children won't suffer. Too much or too little frustration damages a child's hope, and without hope, we find it very hard to continue with life's struggles.

A healthy adult has a balanced, realistic sense of entitlement; and having a clear, well-developed ego, she has the ability to meet many of her needs in appropriate ways. A grown-up woman can look at a frustrating problem and see a challenge and an opportunity. A downturn in one area of her business triggers layers deep inside of her that she hadn't touched in ages, including fear of survival, wants, needs, fear of deprivation, memories of competition with a sister in early childhood, shame, competence and power. After the initial shock and numbness following the bad news begin to wear off, and as the knots in her stomach unwind a little bit, she is able to create new business opportunities by coordinating her creative fantasies with her practical knowledge and ability to act. She doesn't just sit at home, depressed, longing for someone to rescue her or for the business climate to change on its own; and she doesn't just fantasize about other business opportunities that she could pursue without acting on the fantasies. She fantasizes and then makes it happen. There are few experiences more satisfying, rewarding or deepening for an adult than ones like these.

A SILVER SPOON AND AN EMPTY CUP

A man who grew up in a wealthy family came to us with complaints of a troubling existential crisis. He was vaguely depressed, his dreams were diffuse and fitful, he was haunted by a sense of emptiness and an almost ethereal feeling of loss, and he had much difficulty sustaining meaningful relationships. His notable intelligence appeared to be cloaked in a heavy drapery of embarrassment, although he wasn't certain if that was the word he should use to describe it. Stepping back from the surface of this man so that we could begin to perceive what was swirling around in his depths, we were taken by the exquisite beauty of his inner struggle. His soul appeared deep and dark and full with magnificent complexity. On the outside he looked lost, like a child who had been separated from his parents at an amusement park, unable to enjoy the fun surrounding him because he had been cut off from his foundation of safety.

As we explored with him the swirling darkness inside, bits and pieces of his true self began to take shape, asking to be recognized and acknowledged. With each acknowledgment from us came further clarification of what was gnawing away at the edges of his soul. What emerged was a strong, clear voice that spoke of childhood indulgence and overprotection, of a family that had overcome generations of failure and shame, only to recreate it in its opposite form of excessive materialism and insulation from the darkness and pain of the world outside the family compound. The voice spoke of a hunger for struggle, a need for struggle, a longing for struggle, and it also spoke of a fearful unfamiliarity with disappointment, of frustration unknown but powerfully desired.

As his therapy progressed, that voice inside shifted him into action and he made a series of carefully planned decisions that created struggle and stress in his life. He began to embrace struggle, befriend it, learn from it, luxuriate in the exertion that it took to struggle. And then one day this man passed through this door into the soul of adulthood.

Chapter 4

RESISTANCE

Life is but a day: A fragile dewdrop on its perilous way from a tree's summit

John Keats
Sleep and Poetry, 1817

Resistance is an integral part of struggle because without it struggle would not be possible. It is actually resistance that allows us to experience each other and the world around us. This is true in all aspects of the natural world whether in a physical, psychological or spiritual sense. For example, when the wind blows through the Sierra Nevada mountains during a late summer thunderstorm, it produces the most magnificent, mysterious, soulful noise one could possibly hear. It is not quite a whoosh, not quite a howl, not quite a roar, not quite a moan, not quite a sigh. It is rather as if the spectacular granite mountains themselves had breathed in all of creation and then released it back out into the universe in one strong, steady exhale followed by another. As the air passes through the pine trees, it meets resistance from the tree trunks and branches, but it is the resistance that it encounters as it rushes through the millions of delicate pine needles on the trees that accounts for the exquisite sound. Billions of air molecules made up of protons, neutrons and electrons flowing over, under, around and through millions of pine needles. Air molecules colliding with pine needles and pine needles brushing against each other. And together they produce the sound of the heavens breathing, for the splendid enjoyment of all who could appreciate such things.

The answer to the age-old question must therefore be, "There is a sound of one hand clapping, but only because of the resistance the hand meets as it brushes against molecules of air." William Shakespeare wrote that all the world's a stage and each person must play his part, and indeed, all of life's dramas are played out on this stage of resistance. Life requires struggle, and struggle requires resistance.

RELATIONSHIP RESISTANCE

Couples often come to us with resistance dilemmas, although they don't know that at the time. A woman complains that her partner isn't strong enough, masculine enough or that her partner is too much of a milquetoast. A man is angry at his partner for walking away every time they get into a fight. He laments, "Why can't you just hang in there and deal with me face-to-face once in awhile?" Or one person ends a relationship with another because the other was too agreeable, too accommodating, too easy. And at the opposite extreme, many relationships are in trouble because they possess too much resistance, leading the couples to say, "All we ever do is fight and then stubbornly resist each other's overtures for a few days just for good measure, so that it never feels like we're together on much of anything."

On any number of occasions over the years, a man in one of our men's therapy groups finds himself struggling with his passivity and fear of disagreement. Although he is intelligent and understands the value of anger and conflict in keeping relationships alive, he seems unable to act on his insight. Whenever his partner gets angry at him—whether she is justified or not—his only response is to yield and agree, or withdraw. Of course the more he does this the more disappointed and enraged she becomes, so that the next time something happens she is even more intimidating, which makes him even more afraid of her, and so they appear caught in an endless, downward spiral of what some would call passive-aggressiveness. But we prefer to call it a dilemma of resistance—one creates too much, the other too little.

We encourage the more dominant partner to temporarily set aside her anger so that she can get to the vulnerability in the deeper parts of her soul. This is a tremendous risk for her because being in charge has been her edge to keep her from being hurt. The mere thought of sharing power is frightening. At the same time, we begin to help the more yielding partner learn to appreciate the importance of resistance, and then to start providing it.

In men's group it can be a very effective illustration to have the man stand up and face another man, both of them with their arms and hands outstretched, palms forward, touching, so that they can maneuver each other around the room by pushing and yielding. We first have them stand there and simply push and yield with their hands and arms, as if they are getting used to the rudder controls of an airplane. As they get the hang of it, they are unconsciously getting a sense of what cooperative resistance feels like at a deep physical level. Next, we ask the typically passive man to provide no resistance as the other man pushes him around the room, forward, left, right, fast, slow. We stop them and ask the passive man how it feels and he usually says something like, "It's okay," or "It's not too bad," or "I guess I don't like it, I don't know."

Then we ask the passive man to take charge while his partner yields. He appears uncomfortable at first, being unaccustomed to leading in this way, but soon he gets the hang of it and a smile appears at the edges of his mouth as he discovers how good it feels to have some power in relation to another human being. The other group members find themselves filled with grateful relief, because they have been carrying the tension of his passivity and his wife's anger inside of them for as long as he has been in the group. This simple exercise becomes a concrete example for what will eventually happen in his marriage—he and his wife will share the power and thereby match each other's resistances, resulting in gratitude, relief, excitement, energy and contentment.

In *Existential Sexuality*, philosopher Peter Koestenbaum wrote that ". . . the weak and immature, those who are not ready for love, will collapse under the weight of the independence of their beloved." Independence implies resistance because of the boundary around the independent person. It implies that there will be times when I cannot have everything that I want from the other person, leading to healthy frustration and disappointment. The other's independence is a crucial part of love and existence because as Koestenbaum later noted, "*The independence of the other consciousness permanently assures me that I am not alone in this world!*" We cannot help but feel lonely when we are in a relationship with one who does not provide resistance because without resistance the other person becomes invisible.

Some people feel that these ideas of independence and resistance are cold and harsh. Others recognize their truth but feel that they are simply too painful and difficult to attain. Indeed, to accept that we cannot fully possess another human being is frightening at first, because it taps into our natural fear of abandonment. But the tension produced as we try to balance fusion and isolation is what keeps our relationships vibrant over the years. It truly is what separates the numb relationships from the dynamic ones.

German poet Rainer Maria Rilke defined love as ". . . two solitudes that touch and greet and protect each other." Many of us can relate to the last part of the definition, but it is the part about solitude that frightens us. Despite her love for you, an independent person will want time away from you, she will have a part of herself that is just hers, and the moment that she makes the final leap from this world into the next, she will do it alone. People sometimes ask, "Why can't we simply dispense with the 'two solitudes' part of Rilke's definition?" It seems such a trivial difference to argue, but it is far from trivial. It is the difference between the Grand Canyon and a crack in one's driveway—similar in all ways except one, and that one makes all the difference in the universe. If we were not two solitudes there would be no resistance.

In *The Road Less Traveled*, M. Scott Peck wrote that we could not be truly in love with someone unless we could be happy living without them. The resistance present in a deep relationship between two solitudes is exciting, delicate, ecstatic, fragile and energizing. To use Peck's word, it is called "love." When two people have what we call dependency damage, the resistance between them is either so slight that they are mired in emotional muck most of the time, or so strong that they are trapped in intense conflict most of the time. One's outer logic might suggest that we would feel more alive if we swung between the extremes of infantile fusion and infantile rage. But our inner logic tells us that when two people let go of resistance extremes and move toward subtlety, the exquisite tension that results can keep people feeling alive and connected with life and each other for decades. Subtle resistance is a crucial part of both the early sexual chemistry between partners, as well as the long-term emotional passion in their relationship.

The concept of resistance is also helpful in trying to fathom the dynamics of abusive relationships. In a healthy relationship, the overall resistance of one matches the overall resistance of the other, and it is the alternating, subtle yielding of one to the other that accounts for the understated passion that is ever present between the two. She moves towards him and exerts her will just as he willingly yields. He moves towards her and exerts his will just as she willingly yields. This dance of exertion and yielding that is shared and desired and accepted by both partners accounts for the beauty and magic of their love. In an abusive relationship, he moves towards her, exerts his will against her protests, feels that her resistance is a threat to his being, gets scared, exerts his will some more, meets resistance and then flies into a rage with the goal of destroying her resistance altogether. He unwittingly crushes her soul and the soul of the relationship in the process. Infants scream and rage when their fantasies meet resistance. Grown-ups savor the exquisite tension allowed by resistance and thus reap the rewards of having embraced the soul of adulthood.

RESISTANCE IN WORK AND CHARACTER

We hear someone say, "She appreciates it much more because she had to work for it." There is truth in simple statements like these. When everything comes to us without struggle and resistance, we soon grow weary, becoming awash in boredom. Our perceptions of life become distorted. We lose a sense of the subtleties that make life intriguing. We have no awe and wonder anymore. We have little ability to endure. In *A Nation of Victims*, Charles Sykes laments the weakening of our national character, pointing out that we once saw the facing of adversity as that which builds character. He does not argue that we should return to the inhumane days when we denied child abuse, but notes that when we see all adversity as bad we pay the price. Adversity, after all, does build character.

We recall the story of the five-year-old Native American boy who was in a hut with several of the tribal elders when he decided to go outside. As he began to tug on the heavy wooden door to the hut, he discovered it provided a great deal of resistance. It wouldn't budge. He continued to tug, occasionally looking back into the faces of the elders, either for approval of his methods or perhaps hoping that one of them would help him. The elders responded with serious, expressionless faces and said nothing. The little boy persisted in his important work, periodically looking back at the elders, who continued to respond as they had before. At last the door opened and the little boy turned around quickly to see the reaction. The chief, who was the most imposing of them all, looked down at the little boy with strength and dignity and solemnly nodded his approval. With that subtle gesture of acknowledgment, the little boy's spirit soared, and he bounded out onto the prairie to play.

This marvelous story is rich with many meanings, not the least of which is the value of resistance in building character. Time and again, we see overanxious well-meaning parents removing every obstacle from the life paths of their children. A teenager agrees that it is time for him to get a summer job and pay for some of his expenses and then two weeks into it he quits, complaining that the job was boring. Out of pity rather than empathy, the parents pay his car insurance bill and continue to give him spending money, because they don't want him to be uncomfortable. With the obstacle removed, with no resistance in his path, the teenager makes his way through the summer oblivious to the commitment that he made. The parents nag and complain and grill him about how many job interviews he's had that week, but nothing changes because there is no reason for it to change. It is all too easy. No resistance, no incentive, no drive and no character.

In our consulting work with teachers and corporate managers, one of the most consistent problems that arises is that a portion of the students or employees simply lack the will to persist at anything for very long. They often have high intelligence, come from middle-class and upper-middle-class families, have good social skills and appear to have the best of everything in their backgrounds except for these—the ability to meet resistance, struggle with adversity, delay gratification and follow through with long-term plans. It's just too darned hard for them.

By the time these children are the age of adults, the outcomes are very painful. They either remain tied to their parents emotionally and financially, unable to leave the nest and experience the thrill of early adulthood; or they are out on their own but miserable, angry, feeling defeated and filled with shame. When everything is given without resistance, we naturally expect it to stay that way when we grow up.

Never having to reconcile a checkbook, the young adult has no idea of how much money is in his account, and so he bounces checks all over town, destroying his credit rating and getting into legal trouble. He then feels enraged at the stupidity and unfairness of the people who want to be paid for their goods, instead of acknowledging his mistake, correcting it and moving on. He hates authority figures, gives up when he is assigned a challenging term paper in his favorite college class, gets depressed and stops trying after his first job interview doesn't land him the job, and feels that people who don't scrape and bow at his every command are out to get him. The very resistance that makes life invigorating for the resilient young adult makes it unbearable for the young adult whose parents thought they were being so helpful by removing as much resistance as possible.

As we note in the chapter on Struggle, the resistance that a child is allowed to experience should match his age and capabilities. It would be damaging and dangerous to let a four-year-old child stay home by himself while you go out to dinner, but it would be a wonderful challenge for him to learn to tie his shoes, put away his toys at night and learn that he can't have candy bars from the check-out counter at the supermarket.

It is as if these little limits that we bump into as we are growing up partially inoculate us from the damaging stress of the larger resistances we meet after we leave home. Not getting the candy bar when we are four helps us wait until we can afford to buy a car we want when we are 34. Having a definite bedtime that is consistently enforced when we are six helps us to structure our work day when we are 26. Staying home until we have finished our homework when we are 12 helps us to follow through with our commitments when we are 42. And being rejected by a steady date when we are 16 and learning to accept the resistance with dignity, helps keep us from battering our loved ones later on.

As a child samples greater and greater resistances throughout her first 20 years of life, she gradually acquires the confidence and ability to survive in the world. Meeting and struggling with resistance is not just about pine needles brushing together to make a heavenly sound, or about little boys opening heavy wooden doors. It is about the ability to make our way in the world, to have deeply meaningful and fulfilling relationships, and to meet life head-on with faith and hope.

Chapter 5

THE UNCONSCIOUS

A safe but sometimes chilly way of recalling the past is to force open a crammed drawer. If you are searching for anything in particular, you don't find it, but something falls out at the back that is often more interesting.

J.M. Barrie, from the
dedication to his first
edition of *Peter Pan*

A woman sees a man in a crowded room, and her heart picks up its beat just a little bit, unbeknownst to her. Her pupils dilate just a fraction, and there is a subtle shift in her breathing. Chemicals are released into her bloodstream and flow across the synapses in her brain. In her consciousness she becomes aware of her feelings. They approach each other and make eye contact for a fleeting moment. Her heart rate increases, her hands begin to perspire and her breathing stops momentarily. Something is happening unconsciously. As they approach each other they begin to give off literally hundreds of subtle messages. They send tiny cues and signals to each other, with the way they walk, their faces, body posture, eyes, head movements, skin tone, pupil dilation, arms, hands and mouths. Their brains are processing thousands of messages of which they are mostly unaware. As they are processed, they are integrated and summarized into a conscious report that says simply and clearly, "Go forward." The words they first speak are insignificant compared to these other signals. The dance of romance has begun, and the two are barely aware of what has already taken place.

Some people believe that we first became aware of the unconscious parts of ourselves after Sigmund Freud formally integrated his own observations along with those of his contemporaries. It was his systematic description of the unconscious—the dark reservoir of impulses, urges, needs and drives that make up the majority of human personality—that so shocked the rational Victorian Age in which he lived. His discoveries were intriguing but also frightening because we were convinced that in our emerging industrial order we had finally overcome our primitive savagery. In truth, human beings have paid homage to the unconscious from our beginnings over 150,000 years ago. Freud simply wrote about it in analytical terms and metaphors that fit the logical era in which we now live. For as long as we have existed on this planet, we have passed on to later generations our myths, tales, art, poetry, beliefs, and an emphasis on the messages contained in dreams; and each of these is a clear sign of how much we acknowledge and try to listen to our unconscious minds.

Since Freud first wrote about the unconscious, we have become increasingly sophisticated in our understanding of the human brain. We have mapped out the location of many of its functions and identified its basic neurochemistry. And yet no matter how much we dissect, analyze or tinker with the workings of the brain, we will always experience much of our existence at an unconscious level, because to do it any other way would be overwhelming. There is simply too much information that comes to us constantly through our senses. If the man and woman falling in love had to stop to consciously process all of the information that they were transmitting back and forth, they would never get across the room to meet one another. At midnight they would still be saying to themselves, "And then I noticed her eyebrow move up a few millimeters, and then I saw his skin flush just a little, and then I saw her head tilt to the right one degree, and then . . ." It would be absurd. We can drive our automobiles not in spite of the unconscious, but because of it.

WHAT IS IN THE UNCONSCIOUS?

Many people think of the unconscious mind as a fore-boding, barely controllable place inhabited by dark images and malevolent urges. Many of us learned in school that it is our unconscious mind that accounts for the atrocities that we perpetrate upon each other, and that when and if we are able to keep our unconscious minds under control we will have created a truly humane world. As Freud noted, the unconscious contains our darkest fears, urges, fantasies and impulses. A nice quiet boy has violent dreams of killing his father. A respectable wife and mother fanta-sizes having wild, passionate sex with another partner. After an earthquake or tornado wreaks its destruction on a community, the townspeople have nightmares filled with chaos and pain. Someone embarrasses us in front of every-one and out of nowhere we realize we are fantasizing that person's painful demise. Shocked at how uncivilized and disturbing the thoughts are, we quickly take conscious control of them and push them away, perhaps only to see them reappear a few hours later. Freud believed that the unconscious contains our primitive biological urges to survive, and in more literal terms those urges include sexual reproduction, avoidance of damage and pain, connection with our fellow human beings and destruction of other creatures we deem dangerous.

In other words, this container of primitive feelings and images is an essential ally to us, and like an electronic security system, it carries out most of its protective work without our conscious awareness. And it is a magnificent mechanism to say the least. Much of Freud's insight into the unconscious came from his work with people who had what in today's terminology are called dissociative disorders, one of the more dramatic being multiple personality. Some people think about multiple personality disorder as frightening and disturbing, but in the bigger scheme of things it is simply an indication that the human brain is brilliantly adaptive and self-protective. When a child is so terribly hurt that her mental circuits are literally in danger of overloading, the brain simply divides pieces of the trauma into manageable chunks and then builds a separate identity around each of them. We can think of few safety devices that are more elegant and effective than this.

One of the most fascinating aspects of human beings is that the patterns that determine how we live our lives are also largely unconscious, a fact that many people do not want to believe. Day in and day out, we are exposed to thousands of tiny messages in our families, and as those messages are repeated, they begin to form patterns in our minds that run automatically. We see our parents fight fairly and cleanly for years and then in adulthood we find ourselves fighting fairly and cleanly with our friends and loved ones. We witness Dad being cruel to Mom while Mom suffers in silence; we make a vow that we will never get in a relationship like that when we grow up. Years later we discover ourselves suffering in silence as our partner is repeatedly cruel to us, or we discover ourselves being cruel to our partner; but because the pattern is unconscious, we simply don't make the connection.

Human beings are creatures of habit, and habits are stored in the unconscious so that we don't have to use all of our brain capacity to consciously think through everything we do each day. It's not good or bad, it's just the way it works. For people who were exposed to useful patterns in childhood, it is a blessing, and for those who were exposed to troubled patterns, it is difficult. Psychotherapy can be viewed as helping us to identify those patterns and habits so that we can stop repeating them, and replace them with healthier habits. In the beginning of this process, people learn to listen to the subtle messages emanating from the unconscious. As they become more comfortable in the presence of these messages, despite the pain and fear associated with them, people can begin to see those patterns more clearly in their daily lives. They can then prepare to replace them with habits that are better.

The unconscious also contains our hopes and dreams, our fantasies and wishes, our creativity and the very depths of our souls. A woman struggles with the solution to a complicated mathematics problem, sets it aside, and then finds the answer popping into her mind as she drives home from work. A man searches for a new way to explain a difficult concept to his students; upon awakening the next morning he realizes that the answer has come to him in a vivid dream. A boy watches in fear and sadness as his mother agonizes with a chronic disease throughout her life; then years later he graduates from medical school but makes no connection between her condition and his choice to enter the healing arts.

The unconscious isn't just a place of darkness, fear and primitive survival urges. It is also the home of all that is mysterious and beautiful about us. It is a place where our deepest connections with creation begin, where we find the humor and joy in life, where we are able to fathom the ecstasy and depth of the universe. It only scares us because we believe that it is not under our control, and when we feel something is out of control, we become afraid. But if it is an integral part of us, then we have both access to it and the potential to harness the wisdom of what is in it if we are patient, diligent and open to the messages it contains. In *Lucid Dreaming*, a book about dream research at Stanford University, Stephen LaBerge describes people's ability to consciously enter and change the outcome of their dreams, a feat most of us find quite astounding.

HOW DOES THE UNCONSCIOUS SPEAK TO US?

Freud used dream analysis, free association and slips of the tongue as some of the windows to the unconscious. He observed that the material in the unconscious is metaphorical, not literal, and that it is in the form of sensory images rather than being abstracted and consciously interpreted. That is why our dreams can be so perplexing when we first look at them. They aren't logical in a conscious way, but they may be infinitely meaningful if we step back from them long enough to discern their metaphorical depth and meaning. A man told us of a frightening dream in which he was standing beside a great dam that was beginning to crack. As the flood waters surged over the top, the dam broke open and water burst forth in a raging torrent. The man said he was frightened by the dream, but that it was also exciting to see all of that power being released at one time. The dream is interesting in and of itself, but much more so when observed in light of the sexual impotence with which the man struggled.

The unconscious sensory images that accompany love, warmth, closeness, distance, violence, hunger, poverty and want are powerful, and they enter into our souls whether we want them there or not. They simply are. And because they are primitive and uninterpreted by our higher cortical centers, we often dismiss them as mere foolishness—just the brain firing randomly to clear its circuits for the next day's work. But they are often much more than that. The man in chapter 1 who struggled with where he wanted to live found himself flooded with sensory images that came to him in his dreams and in his waking reality:

My more peaceful childhood memories constantly tweak and poke and prod me with hypnotically deep sensory impressions of soft, warm, dry summer air infused with the earthy scent of eucalyptus and bay laurel. As I breathe the memories deeper and deeper into my soul, the smell of the

hot dry, powdery earth mixed with manzanita and sage
surround me, engulf me, take command of my being.

At one level we could say that he simply longed for the place where he grew up. At another level we could say that he longed for the warmth, safety and internal peace that we all desire, regardless of where we live, and that the harmony he felt in nature was something that he wanted in other parts of his life as well.

The unconscious speaks to us in many ways other than dreams. The man and woman who found themselves attracted to each other at the beginning of this chapter weren't drawn towards each other randomly. The people with whom we fall in love fit some kind of pattern that is already known to us at some level. It is said that we marry people like our mothers or fathers, which is true if by this we mean that the patterns are similar. If we grew up in a family with a lot of conflict we will probably be drawn to one extreme or the other—i.e., a person with whom we can be in conflict much of the time, or a person who unconsciously agrees with us that any conflict is bad. In either extreme, the relationship will be fraught with difficulty.

A woman discovered that she had spent most of her adulthood consciously trying hard to be the opposite of her mother, who was very much caught in the pleasing victim role. Mom was sweet, gentle, quiet and passive while Dad was domineering, critical and demanding. The woman grew up vowing to be different. She grew a shell of toughness around her and saw any attempt to correct her or instruct her as a sign of domination. Consequently, she was constantly butting heads with teachers and later with supervisors at work. She filed lawsuits at the drop of a hat, believing that the world was filled with people who were out to deprive her of her human rights. She was humorless, angry, controlling, domineering and unhappy. To ensure that she didn't have a marriage like her mother's, she fell in love with a quiet, gentle, passive, yielding man with whom she consciously felt safe, but whom she unconsciously resented for his lack of independence and resistance. In her overzealously conscious attempt to avoid being like her mother, she had unconsciously bonded more with her father's traits and had married her mother instead. When we speak of meeting a man or woman whom we feel we have known deeply in some other time or place, we believe it may often be due to these unconscious patterns.

The unconscious speaks to us all the time. When we get home at night and become aware that we have been grinding our teeth all day or have painful neck and shoulder muscles, it is often a message that we have been afraid during the day, which is what negative stress is actually about. A woman has recurrent panic attacks and discovers in therapy that she has been holding inside years of emotions that are longing to be acknowledged and released. A man gets angry whenever his partner threatens to leave the relationship, but as he listens to his unconscious, as he goes beneath the surface of his outer self to discover what is beneath, he finds that he is more deeply afraid, hurt, sad and lonely than angry. As he gains insight and maturity, he will later be able to see his urge to rage as a possible road sign that there is something more vulnerable and more true underneath, and that if he shares it with his partner now and then, the partner might not want to leave after all.

When we suggest that people keep a journal as part of their healing process, we also suggest that the journal be kept in a safe place so that it can be used as an avenue into the unconscious. We encourage people to write whatever comes to them in whatever form it is revealed, which means that a woman who dearly loves her partner may write about how much she hates her partner in the moment. Those unconscious feelings and urges are not bad, they are simply who we are at the time, and we can learn from them if we listen. We do painful things to ourselves and others when we deny what is inside of us— when we are so afraid to admit the feeling that we pretend it isn't there. People who batter their infants are so ashamed that they never share the urges with anyone; whereas, people who don't batter their infants can admit that under stress we are all capable of feeling like we could batter. Non-batterers know that sharing a feeling with someone can take away its destructive power while giving an opportunity to channel constructive power into useful coping skills. To feel something isn't damaging; it's what we do with the feeling that can hurt.

Listening to your feelings is as important as realizing that you don't have to act on them. The unconscious is not a literal road map. Some people create tremendous pain for themselves and others because they are unable to distinguish between their unconscious feelings and reality. Just because you feel like doing or not doing something doesn't mean you are betraying your true self if you don't act on the feeling. Just because you may feel like everyone is out to get you doesn't mean that everyone is. The unconscious is especially frightening to us if we take it literally.

If we let it speak to us, if we play with its metaphors and images rather than accepting them as literal truth, then there is much to be gained from this most mysterious and wondrous entryway into the soul of adulthood.

Chapter 6

ENTITLEMENT

It is happy for human nature that there are desires which cannot be satisfied. Otherwise, the most sorry man would make himself master of the world.

Stanislaus Leszcynski
Oeuvres du philosophe bienfaisant, 1763

Over 100 years ago, Alexis De Tocqueville described Americans as "forever brooding over advantages they do not possess . . . It is strange to see with what feverish ardor the Americans pursue their own welfare, and to watch the vague dread that constantly torments them lest they should not have chosen the shortest path which may lead to it." Tocqueville's observation was brilliant, and what he described continues to be one of the more disturbing neurotic symptoms that plague Americans today. It goes something like this: "I want it all, right now, with or without effort, and if I don't get it, I want to make someone pay for my unhappiness." While citing Tocqueville's quote in *A Nation of Victims,* Charles Sykes notes that "residents of the Old World, in far less advantageous circumstances, tended not to dwell on their misfortunes." In other words, when compared to our European ancestors, our distorted sense of entitlement is cause for considerable embarrassment.

TO WHAT ARE WE ENTITLED?

Questions of entitlement are confusing for many of us, and learning to balance the important elements of disappointment, struggle and entitlement is crucial in opening the doors to adulthood. Are we entitled to own our own home? Are we entitled to a certain income? To medical care? To owning a video camera? Are we entitled to be happy?

We like to believe that a newborn infant has certain inalienable rights, but in reality, while we may be entitled to good care when we are young and vulnerable, it is only through the benevolence and accountability of our caregivers that good care is received. As infants and youngsters, we truly are at the mercy of those who hold sway over our lives, and so it is purely by the luck of the draw that we are born into a family, rich in resources, which treats us well and which honors our longings to live. But we feel entitled to live whether we will or not.

As we move out of early infancy, and if our basic needs are met moderately well, then our sense of self, our uniqueness, starts to form and we begin to put our special imprint on the world around us. At the same time, we begin to develop desires beyond those of simple biological survival—we begin to want certain things that become expressions, manifestations and symbols of our emerging self. A child sees a toy and something about it resonates with his spirit. It fascinates, entices, holds out the hope and promise of challenge, play, intrigue and joy. The child decides that he wants it. Now, rather than simply struggling to stay biologically alive, the child becomes engaged in a struggle to form, mold, build, strengthen, extend and express his psychological self. Many experts describe our "wants" as those things that define our uniqueness and our spiritedness. The things that capture our attention, like the toy, help to define who we are separate from others. You want this toy and I want that toy. We resonate to different aspects of the world because we are different.

Some adults who have not learned to struggle well, and who did not have their basic needs met well in childhood, remain trapped in infancy so that they can't tell the difference between their internal feelings and external reality. The line between the two remains blurred, and they actually believe that it must be real if they feel it. This is a simple but accurate description of the struggle facing someone with Borderline Personality Disorder, whose life is in constant chaos, and whose behavior is dictated almost entirely by the unpredictable swings of emotion that we all experience. A healthy adult has emotional ups, downs, nuances and fluctuations throughout the day but learns to judge with wisdom and care which feelings should be acted upon, so while at one moment she might feel like hurting someone, she realizes that these emotions are to be felt and listened to rather than acted out or expressed.

Other adults who have had unhealthy frustration in infancy learn the lesson too well and develop such a rigid boundary between internal feelings and external reality that they defer their own gratification no matter what, constantly depriving themselves of what they want and need. They live a sterile life of over-control and deprivation, never honoring those deep longings that stir at the core of their souls. They assume that they will never get anything that they want, and so they don't even ask. In other words, children who are deprived and children who are spoiled will share deep, painful struggles around entitlement and definition of self.

TWO GIRLS AND A BOY

We knew two women who shared similar struggles surrounding their desires. One wanted an expensive European sedan but didn't have the money to buy it. Despite the advice she sought from friends and relatives, she leased the automobile and enjoyed it immensely for about nine months, until she was no longer able to make the payments on it. It was only through the volunteer legal help of a close relative that she was able to avoid personal bankruptcy, and she was profoundly disappointed when she had to surrender the car. The other woman wanted a reasonably priced American sports coupe, and although she had created a very successful business and certainly had the money to afford such a purchase, she continued to drive her eight-year-old station wagon with the broken radio because deep inside of her there remained a message that she didn't deserve the luxury of a new car with a good sound system. Both women had issues about entitlement, and for seemingly opposite reasons, the end result for both of them was the same.

A young man graduated from college with a degree in business and landed his first job after only two interviews, which strengthened his deep internal belief that he was blessed in ways that others were not. He worked hard, learned quickly and received an excellent performance review after six months on the job, but then he discovered that he was frequently bothered by thoughts and feelings that he could not contain. He had absorbed much of what he could know about his entry level position, and he found himself growing bored and dissatisfied with his work. He began to create elaborate proposals which he would enthusiastically present to his supervisor. His supervisor would read each proposal and discuss it with the young man, praising him for his creativity, and explaining that it took time for major changes like these to be incorporated into the long-term plan of a big organization like theirs. The young man would listen, trying to be patient, but he became increasingly frustrated, believing that his supervisor was stodgy, rigid and afraid to take the risks necessary to get ahead in business.

His supervisor went out of his way to tell the president of the corporation what a shining star the young man was turning out to be. The president was pleased, telling the supervisor that if the young man continued to excel after 18 months, he would then be eligible for early promotion, an honor bestowed on very few employees. But the young man had always gotten what he wanted pretty much when he felt he should, and because he had always worked hard and been smart, he had always felt entitled. So, nine months into his new job, the young man began to act on his feelings despite all he had learned in college.

He gradually criticized the management of the corporation until he located other employees who were dissatisfied with one little thing or another, and then he escalated his criticism, mistakenly believing that he had enough political support to push his changes through. He fervently believed he was right and became indignant. His supervisor shared the president's plans for early promotion in the hopes that it was just a matter of youthful impatience needing to be tempered by reality, but by now the young man was such a prisoner of his feelings that nothing helped. He became angrier, more demanding, more critical and more destructive to the goals of the company, until one day he was simply fired. There was nothing else to be done.

WHAT IS ENOUGH?

America is a practical nation as evidenced by the cleverness of so many of our national heroes. We like to view America as being founded by pioneers, inventors and entrepreneurs, people with boundless optimism, willingness to take incredible risks and an attitude of success. We like to think we still have no limits or resistance, as perhaps many of our forefathers believed as they marched ever westward, moving through the Appalachian forests, across the Mississippi Valley and the Great Plains, over the Rocky Mountains, and into California. Yes, on the one hand these people faced incredible odds, risked their lives and struggled valiantly to build a new nation. But on the other hand, we sacrificed parts of our souls to do it. We looked the other way while our armies destroyed the native peoples, or we justified it in the name of our god. We were so intent on exploring, conquering and building that as we ran toward the west coast we ran away from ourselves. Almost from the time of Columbus 500 years ago, we have been a nation of people who have led each other to believe that we can have it all.

What is enough? It is hard to say. Sometimes the only way we find out this soulful truth is when life stops us dead in our tracks. When the Challenger space shuttle blew up in the bright blue sky, we witnessed the unraveling of our myths about our own perfection. After years of nearly flawless spaceflights, we discovered a host of design and launch control flaws that had been lurking just beneath the surface waiting to reveal how real our human limits are. It was a sobering way to learn that we can't have it all, as was the Vietnam War, Watergate and any of the other tragedies that have befallen our nation.

Life places limits on us, and while life and liberty should be part of any healthy society, the pursuit of happiness means just that—the right to pursue happiness but with no guarantee that we will always find it and keep it. Entitlement and disappointment go hand-in-hand. Our nation has so many freedoms built into it that some would say we are neurotic because of those freedoms. If that is so, then we are like children who have no bedtime, who can stay out as late as we want, use any drugs or chemicals that we want, take anything we want from anyone we want, and have a marvelous time doing it until life stares us squarely in the eyes and says, "It's time for you to learn your limits."

We had the right idea in trying to dispense with the social caste system that exists in the many cultures from whence we came, but maybe we went too far. For while it is true that nearly anyone can grow up in America and become a millionaire, it is also true that many people will never get out of abject poverty in this country. We suspect that for every self-made millionaire there are thousands more out there who have died trying, unsuccessfully, to get to financial Nirvana before their neighbors do, just as Tocqueville described it over 100 years ago.

It is said that between two healthy adults, whatever they can give each other at the time is enough. We tend to agree with the spirit of this belief but acknowledge that there are times when it is hard to live up to it. A man wants his wife to stay home one evening because he just received some painful or frightening news but she can't because of an equally pressing commitment. His wife conveys her compassion for him and regretfully leaves, returning later to share his struggle with him. A woman wants more of a relationship with her friend than the friend is able or willing to give. The friend is honest and respectful of her feelings, but is clear about where the limits are for her. If they are in adulthood, the man and woman above who don't get all that they want will graciously accept the limit placed on them by the other rather than nagging or manipulating. As adults they trust that they can still be okay and that they have other options if needed. The man may call a couple of friends or relatives and share the painful news with them. The woman feels the sting of not having her feelings reciprocated but goes forward to establish a closer friendship with someone else. People are like life. Sometimes we simply aren't able to give each other what we want when we want it.

STAGES OF ENOUGH

Some social commentators have described the 1980s as a decade of greed and self-absorption, during which the prevailing moral and economic mood was to take as much as you can regardless of who gets hurt. Perhaps. But regardless of which decade we examine, when people are coming to terms with their own personal definition of what is enough, they seem to go through similar stages regardless of how much they actually have.

The first is a state of fearing that we will never have enough. This is like being under siege emotionally or financially and is felt as near-constant deprivation and desperation. A man who has many shortages from childhood may believe that he will never get enough love and support from friends and family. A woman who grew up in wealth fears that she will never be able to match her parents' income, thus feeling deprived despite her respectable salary.

The second is a state in which we fear that we will always have just enough—that we will make it from day-to-day or month-to-month, but that deprivation is lurking just outside the door. "My wife loves me dearly," he says, "but just enough. One tiny shift in any direction and I'll be right back in a state of desperation again." Needless to say, these first two stages carry a great deal of anxiety.

One might think that getting to the third stage means having so much that we couldn't possibly ever be in deprivation again, but that would be a destructive childish fantasy. So, being in this third stage could only mean one thing—that we can truly appreciate what we do have.

Because of the historical dynamics mentioned earlier in this chapter, we believe that getting to this third stage is one of the greatest challenges that faces Americans today and into the next century. If a man or woman can say that they deserve a vacation in Hawaii this year but it will have to wait because they can't afford it, and if they can accept that limitation and truly be grateful for what they do have instead of bemoaning what they don't, then they have successfully passed through the next door to the soul of adulthood.

Chapter 7

DISAPPOINTMENT

Oft expectation fails, and most oft there
Where most it promises, and oft it hits
Where hope is coldest and despair most fits.

William Shakespeare
All's Well That Ends Well, c. 1602

It is not possible to move forward into adulthood without risk, and with risk comes failure, with failure comes disappointment, and with disappointment come clarity and depth. Life's truth tells us that disappointment happens because we care, so when something doesn't turn out the way we'd like, it is natural and sometimes good. If everything we attempted had to turn out perfectly the first time we tried, then the wondrous creations of our many civilizations would never have come to be. There would be no art, no religion, no technology, no medicine, no philosophy, no printing presses or books. If each person was allowed only one chance to fall in love and find the right life partner, perhaps five percent of us would do so. Our disappointment affirms that we are present, full of spirit, engaged in life, trying, wanting something, and that our inner self is speaking. It deepens us, and every once in awhile, it brings gifts of immeasurable joy.

THE MAN, THE WOMAN AND THE SEA

We recall the story of the man and woman we know well who had been together for several years and were creating a deep and abiding love for one another. They had shared many a struggle and many a joy. The man told her how much fun he and his brother and sister had swimming in the ocean every summer, and how important water had become to him during his childhood. The woman shared with him her fear of water, and of how her father had not been a very good swimming teacher because of his impatience and gruffness. But swimming outdoors in cold clear lakes and thundering ocean surf had become so deeply embedded in the man's soul that he was secretly disappointed that the woman wasn't as excited as he was about it.

They discussed these things for several years but always came to the same frustrating conclusion. The woman did not like swimming and felt misunderstood and angry, and deep inside, the man felt betrayed by her reluctance. He kept trying to get her to change because he was convinced that their relationship would be ruined if she was never able to join him in the ocean as his brother and sister had.

One day when they were at the beach on a fairly calm day, the man tried every trick he could think of to talk the woman into going into the ocean with him. Finally, the woman agreed; as they began to walk into the surf, a swell came out of nowhere and washed over them, forcing water into her breathing passages. When he saw the terror in her eyes, the man felt awful, and he vowed to himself and to her that he would never pressure her like that again. The woman saw the remorse in the man's eyes and heard the sincerity in his voice, and the shared instant of simultaneous vulnerability swept over them like a wave of healing light.

The next morning as he was swimming in the surf below their hotel room, he waved to her as she read the morning newspaper and sipped her coffee on the balcony, and she smiled and waved back. And then from nowhere and everywhere inside of him hundreds of disconnected pieces suddenly gathered and formed into an image of completion. He realized that when he was a child, all of that time spent in the boiling surf, or in the cool, dark, mystical water underneath the waves, was his way of soothing the fear and hurt that he frequently felt in his family, and that the secrets he shared with his brother and sister were not just about the ocean and its magical healing properties. As his mind eased back into the here and now, all of those disconnected fragments of pain and confusion were transformed into a single, deep, focused feeling of peace. He realized that the pain of his childhood was behind him, and the beautiful mystery of his relationship with this woman did not demand retreat into a watery sanctuary. He no longer needed someone in the ocean with him to ease his pain. It was enough to swim by himself, and to simply love her.

LIFE, DEATH AND DISAPPOINTMENT

Our literature, oral histories and religions are filled with the value of disappointment in tempering and deepening our souls. The Bible, Talmud, Koran, Greek and Roman mythology, Native American spiritual wisdom, Freudian psychology and authors from Shakespeare to

Robert Bly and Thomas Moore all embrace the importance of trials and tribulations, rituals of initiation and awakening, in our quest for meaning and maturity. Our most important connections to life are often the simplest ones which come only after prolonged struggles that temper, clarify and deepen our souls, and they are therefore earned rather than deserved.

A man says, "I deserve to have the things I want in life. I deserve to be treated well by others. I deserve to be praised for my work. I deserve to be loved. I deserve to have someone pay when things don't work out." It is certainly true that we deserve some things in life, but when we have a distorted sense of entitlement we get terribly confused, believing that some force in life is out to hurt us when we don't get all that we want when we want it. The inability to find the perspective between reality and our desires can result in deeply felt misery and the experience of continual betrayal. An adult with this distortion may become demanding, self-absorbed and manipulative, because he believes that he should be happy all the time, which is impossible for anyone.

As an adult struggles with issues of distorted entitlement, she is invited into the clarifying challenge of coming to terms with her disappointment, which when embraced, permits her to turn a frustrating, scary, miserable life into a full, satisfying, peaceful one. No matter how smart we are, or how wealthy, clever or powerful, life will always offer us the chance to become full through our disappointments. They are some of the primary threads that are woven into our lives; without them, our lives would lack brilliance and definition.

Look into the eyes of a very old woman who has struggled with life, relished in its ecstasy and come to terms with all of its depth, harshness, forgiveness and yielding. Her face may be creased with twists and turns that tell a multitude of stories about childhood insecurities, painful first loves, children born and friends dying, a lover beyond all imagination, missed opportunities, risks well-chosen, losses embraced with grace and dignity, tolerance and wisdom purely earned. Her eyes, while fading, are bright with all that they have taken in, and her soul is full and ready for the next challenge. This gives her peace. She is a living testament to the value inherent in facing disappointment with patience and courage. Even in our fast-moving high technology world, we can still find the precious core of awe when we come face-to-face with an aged soul who has lived well. Few experiences reveal as much power to us.

When someone is touched by grace as he nears life's end, it is especially poignant. An old man we knew had lived a hard, lonely life forged during the Great Depression and strengthened in its isolation by a difficult marriage and alienation from his children. He had never honored the darkness in his soul that had kept him from celebrating his children's birthdays and life transitions, which resulted in an unspoken chasm between him and those he fathered and raised. One day, a few years before he died, this man watched as his daughter's home filled with friends who came to surprise his grandson for his birthday. Even with 30 teenagers noisily celebrating, his tears were easily noticed and welcomed as warmly as his grandson's guests. He didn't stay at the party very long because he grew weary easily, but that mattered little. The gift that he needed to give and receive—to acknowledge his disappointment after so many years of pretending that none existed—had been manifested and accepted. It was enough.

Disappointment completes and fulfills our sacred compact with life—that life will provide as long as we struggle, as long as we try and as long as we are open to receiving gifts from unexpected places. Because of this, the ability to face disappointment gracefully is one of the finest capacities of human beings. One of the hallmarks of the soul of adulthood is the simple recognition that life rarely turns out exactly as we had planned, and that if it does, we are probably living in a shallow delusion that has been carefully constructed out of our earliest fears. Efforts to exert untempered, unrestricted control over life tell us that we are not yet adults, even if our bones creak and our muscles ache from the ripening of age. As we open this door to adulthood and pass through it, we come to find that life is more than we ever imagined when we were young.

Disappointment creates the fire and passion in our struggles. It presents the challenges, it offers the humility and it creates the canvas for our souls to find expression. As we expand ourselves out into the world, we reach for parts of creation that were once beyond our grasp. A child tries to bake a cake for the first time only to find that it has fallen flat. An idealistic young man identifies with a political candidate and offers his boundless energy to help get him elected, only to find that the candidate is as tarnished and flawed as his opponent. A middle-aged woman takes a new position in a highly regarded corporation, only to find that her department has much of the same political stress and petty intrigue as her previous one. After two marriages, a man believes that he has finally discovered the perfect mate, but finds that his third marriage also contains conflicts and painful disappointments.

Feeling let down is a natural part of life's intimate rhythms, and so those examples are nothing more than the ebb and flow of life itself. There is nothing strange about a cake falling flat, a candidate being human or a marriage having conflict. They are the ordinary occurrences in the lives of normal human beings, and they will always be a part of life. A child believes that her heroes are perfect, because this is how the mind of a child works, and so it is perfectly normal for her to believe that life is this simple. Her childhood heroes are omnipotent and morally flawless because she sees the world in this way. It is the gracious acceptance of a hero's flaws that signals a door opening into the soul of adulthood.

Aside from the personal fear of one's death that emerges from deep inside most of us in middle age, nothing is as painful as the disappointments that we face along the way. A man's first marriage ends with such pain and grief that he wonders if he will ever stop hurting. A woman loses her first child in a miscarriage and feels as if her very soul has been torn from inside of her. The career that you thought would be the perfect one for time immemorial turns out to have limitations. The thought of starting over is demoralizing at first, and yet it is the acceptance and embracing of these ordinary losses that eventually heals our fear of death, allowing us to finally live our lives with a peace that we never thought was possible.

Life, death and disappointment are inextricably connected, and in the soul of an adult they rest comfortably together in a state of coherence and peace. When we reach out for something and it eludes us, we encounter the truth of our limitations and our mortality. Our wanting, our desiring, our passion for life can only be felt with depth when we feel the firm and gentle resistance that life provides for us. This resistance is a gift that is only fully appreciated in death, but we are allowed glimpses of it when we feel the twinges and pangs of the little deaths that happen each time we discover that life is not exactly the way we would like it to be.

A man who is still a child will be plagued by inner turmoil each time he discovers that he is surrounded by imperfect human beings and an imperfect world. He will either revile or idolize each person he meets, and those whom he idolizes will eventually fall prey to his painful need for perfection. Over and over, he will find someone to idealize, his unconscious mind will quickly begin searching for flaws until this latest hero has fallen from grace, leaving another void of disappointment in the soul of the beholder. A man who has passed through the door to adulthood will see the limitations, feel the disappointment, accept his hero's flaws, release his need for perfection and then acknowledge his hero's gifts. This lets the hero become a human being with value and dignity while allowing the beholder to be realistic and appreciative, and in the process, the beholder comes a little closer to finding peace with the thought of his own death.

So it seems that it is not always in our best interests to achieve the happiness that we are seeking in the moment. Some people struggle and fight so fiercely at one level of existence that they prevent themselves from moving to the next level of existence where the waters are so much smoother and clearer. Coming to terms with our disappointments isn't always a matter of keeping a stiff upper lip and pushing our pain deep inside so that we can maintain an aura of grace while we are secretly bleeding. It is actually quite ordinary to appreciate what we do not have for the simple reason that by doing so we can be invited down into a deeper level of existence, beyond the surface struggles in which we had become so embroiled. When we are able to do this, life suddenly seems simpler, brighter, deeper, richer and more complex all at the same time.

In the story of the man, the woman and the sea, their struggle with the frustrations and disappointments about each other was rewarded with a brilliant flash of mutual vulnerability that deepened their love in a way that surprised both of them. For a long time the man believed that his relationship with the woman would be doomed unless she eventually relented and took up ocean swimming with him, only to find that their relationship became a lifetime of love because she didn't. The result of their struggle was unpredictable, unplanned and uncontrolled, demonstrating that life is full of wondrous twists and turns that can deepen us and bring us joy in ways we never imagined. However, we must be willing to risk and reach out for what we want at the time, struggle hard, and then let go to leave room for something even better.

As we find true peace in disappointments along the way, the inevitability of our own death loses its terror, which allows us to embrace and fully enjoy life.

Chapter 8

SELF-ESTEEM MYTHS

It is easier to increase in dignity than to acquire it in the first place.

Publilius Syrus
Sententiae, c. 50 B.C.

The self-esteem movement as it has been played out in the United States is perhaps one of the more confusing issues for many of us, and it is probably safe to say that this particular door to the soul of adulthood hasn't always been there. Our need to feel valued and worthy has been there since we first became human, but the need to debunk self-esteem myths is the result of more recent developments in our culture. As with many movements and fads around the globe, this one has led to some rather quaint, if not downright odd, thinking about the nature of human behavior. It isn't that the original premises were out of line, it's just that we seem to have strayed into extremes in our zeal to build our children's self-esteem.

The net result is troubling. For example, in math and science, American school children rank themselves at the top of the heap when compared to other children around the world, which means that they have very high self-appraisal and self-worth. This is wonderful except for the fact that our children consistently rank somewhere between eleventh and fifteenth when compared to other children worldwide. In other words, when it comes to math and science our children are pumped up with so much hot air that they could probably fly. This is a sad state of affairs, because while it is indeed important to build the self-esteem of a child, it isn't healthy to build it with no foundation.

WHEN CHILDREN ARE PRAISED TOO MUCH

When children are not acknowledged for their accomplishments, or when they are constantly criticized, the true self deep inside does not grow enough resulting in low self-esteem. Praise and recognition are essential nutrients for a child's sense of worth, and many children grow up in families that are so limited in emotional resources that there isn't much room for praise. But some children grow up in families with just the opposite problem. Just as too much fertilizer can kill the flowers in your garden, too much praise can kill the spirit inside of a child.

We once directed the practicum portion of a college pre-school where our students could get course credit for working with the children. The preschoolers ranged in age from three to five and were from various socioeconomic backgrounds, the majority being middle class. Different children stood out for different reasons. The ones who were overly aggressive and destructive were perhaps the most obvious. The extremely bright or talented ones stood out as well. And then there were the ones who had obviously been praised for everything they did from morning until night, from sneezing to drawing a picture to eating their lunch. We could almost see their mothers and fathers standing over them like vigilant seagulls guarding the nest, pacing, wondering, worrying, ever more aware of the tiny accomplishments of their child, and ever more ready to praise whatever the child did.

While this might seem like a good way to build up large reserves of self-esteem in a child, the real result is that the child never builds up any sense of personal accomplishment from the inside. It is essential for a child to learn how to struggle and achieve something for the simple reason that he wants to do it. When there is too much praise, the child becomes dependent on the praise rather than on the felt sense that he has done something that provided difficulty and challenge. Many psychologists believe that human beings have an internal need for mastery—that struggling and doing something well in the face of life's resistance is a reward in itself. This need for mastery can thus be frustrated by too many external rewards.

These over-praised preschoolers showed up in class expecting the world to operate like home, but it doesn't. One little boy couldn't persist at anything unless an adult was standing over him showering him with praise every second; a little girl would start to draw a picture and then look around and wait for the adult praise. It was very sad, which is why these children stood out so much. If one of our students wasn't right there to praise the children, they would simply give up and either cry or begin to whine or act out, disrupting everyone around them. These children were suffering from a severe lack of self-esteem, low tolerance for frustration and a tragic inability to delay gratification. It was only through painful and embarrassing conferences with their parents, as well as frustrating struggles at school, that these children were able to be weaned from the praise and begin to enjoy life's challenges from the inside out.

THE FIRST SELF-ESTEEM MYTH

Self-esteem is the result of two major factors. The first is all of the messages that we receive about ourselves as we are growing up, and the second is the development of that internal sense of mastery and competence which we believe is present in each human being. When viewed from this perspective, self-esteem is not some entity inside of us that causes us to act in certain ways, it is simply a way of summarizing these other two factors. When a woman says that she doesn't feel good about herself because she has low self-esteem, it is redundant and fairly meaningless because part of the definition of low self-esteem is that we don't feel good about ourselves. It is a circular statement similar to that of the man who says he'd feel happier if he weren't depressed. Of course he'd be happier if he weren't depressed, because feeling unhappy is part of the definition of depression.

While this may seem like intellectual hair-splitting, it is actually a crucial distinction to make if a person with low self-esteem ever wants to change. When we say we feel bad *because we have low esteem,* there is a deeply embedded unconscious message that our only way out is to get high self-esteem, as if it were something we could buy at the local convenience store. Imagine walking into that store and asking for two gallons of self-esteem. It doesn't work that way. Looking at self-esteem this way encourages us to remain helpless and to feel defeated because it doesn't offer us any way to improve—*it only identifies that a problem exists,* and it does so in a pseudo-technical way that permits us to believe that we're really getting somewhere.

Labeling a problem is the first step toward improvement, not the final step. Therefore, the first self-esteem myth is the statement that "I would feel better about myself if only I had high self-esteem." It makes more clinical sense to say, "I would feel better about myself if I developed some competencies and if I found people in my life who valued me."

THE SECOND SELF-ESTEEM MYTH

Perhaps because of the proliferation of books and seminars on affirmations, or because of our American desire to do it all by ourselves without anyone's help, many people believe that they must pull themselves up by their bootstraps and get all of their self-esteem "from within." A man we know spent several years reading affirmation books and doing affirmations in front of the mirror every day in an admirable attempt to build his self- esteem, as if he were building big muscles by lifting weights. When we asked him how it was working out for him, he sighed dejectedly and said he still felt pretty bad about himself. And when we asked if he was doing anything to get praise from the people around him, he protested, "What good would that do? I have to learn to get all of my self-esteem from within. That's what all the books say."

This is the second self-esteem myth: "I must get all of my esteem from within." It turns out that what he was referring to was the problem that some people have in becoming dependent on the evaluations of others. It is true that some people care too much about what others think, but to go to the other extreme and deny our need for approval is equally unproductive. As we gently challenged this man's belief that he had to do it all by himself, he gradually got out from in front of his mirror and took the risk to be with other people again, emotionally. The difficult part of doing this comes when we encounter those who don't value us, which will always happen. The challenge is to continue meeting more and more people in various situations until we begin to find those who like us just for who we are. Over a two-year period this man was finally able to find some of those people.

As we continued to work with him, he shared his embarrassment about being deficient in many ways when compared to his peers. He didn't play any sports, he didn't have musical talents, he didn't have any interests or hobbies to speak of, and he hadn't done very well in school, although it was quite clear that he was intelligent. It also became clear that no one had ever taken the time to help him develop his competencies, and so that became the focus of the next stage of his work.

Because the desire for mastery comes from within, it was important for him to find that genuine spark of desire deep inside of his soul. After several sessions of exploration, he realized that we truly believed he could learn something new, and our faith in him gave him the boost that he needed. His face lit up with excitement as he blurted out, "I know what I want to learn! I've always wanted to learn how to fly an airplane! But I've always assumed that I didn't have the ability!" And so over the next six months, with the help of a flying instructor, this man learned how to fly—both literally and figuratively.

THE ROOTS OF SELF-ESTEEM

As the man above found out, the paradox of building self-esteem is that *we must do it by ourselves with the help of others.* The drive, spark, fire, energy, enthusiasm, excitement, interest, mystery, wonder, need, desire, hope and effort must come from within us. It must come from the very core of our souls, from our unique perceptions and genetic intricacies, from our drive to comprehend and understand our universe and ourselves. No one can make us become internally competent and have high self-esteem. We can be forced to learn many things, and we can be seduced into saying that we feel good about ourselves even if we don't, but the force of genuine self-esteem comes from our true self.

At the same time, human beings are social animals, and so we need the approval of each other to feel right with the world. We need our parents, teachers and other adults to see and acknowledge us. We need to be loved simply for who we are. It is vitally important for a child to come home after school and be greeted and recognized, not just to be grunted at and fed as if she were one of the family pets. We also need to be taught, challenged and praised for what we do. It isn't enough to unconditionally love a child. There is more that is needed.

If a child is born into a family where she is wanted, valued and appreciated, and where she is acknowledged when she is around her family, where she is just as important as the males in the family, where she is allowed to be an introvert or extrovert depending on her biological gifts, where it is wonderful that she is artistic unlike her scientific sister and her logical brother, where adults teach her things and enjoy seeing her become independent, and where she is encouraged to develop her own lifestyle and values along with the basic decency and humanity that she is taught, then she will grow up to have high self-esteem. If that same child is raised in a family where someone is secretly disappointed that she is a girl, worried because she is an extrovert, displeased because she likes art and music rather than science and math, rarely acknowledges that she exists, doesn't teach her anything or makes learning painful and shaming, tries to keep her dependent for fear of losing her, and doesn't encourage her to develop her own lifestyle and values, then she will have low self-esteem when she grows up.

Adults who had the good fortune of getting their self-esteem reserves filled during childhood must still act to maintain that esteem. It doesn't just stay where it is. A very competent woman with high self-esteem gave a presentation at a conference one day that did not go well. She was "off" and she knew it halfway through the talk. Her self-esteem was bruised by the end of the day as she listened to the last pained attempts by her colleagues to cheer her up. But having good esteem, the drain on her self was tolerable. The next time she gave a presentation she made certain that she was doubly prepared and the talk went flawlessly, and so the part of her esteem that was tied in with her professional competence was again filled up.

ADULT SELF-ESTEEM

Adult self-esteem means that we know what we are good at and what we aren't good at. High esteem doesn't mean grandiosity and arrogance. It does not mean that we deny our limitations. Indeed, a healthy adult will be clear about his shortcomings, even admitting his embarrassment about them. But he will also be clear about his strengths, will be proud of them and will be able to accept compliments about them graciously without the false humility often shown by someone with low esteem. Adults with high esteem truly see challenges as opportunities rather than threats. They continue wanting to learn and to master more about life, not out of some maniacal desire to control the world or out of some frenzied competitive need to be better than anyone else, but because it feels good to learn and do new things, and because the spirit inside of their souls is filled with enthusiasm about life.

And of course, people with high self-esteem make healthier choices about the people they befriend. A woman with low esteem came to us complaining that all of her friends were either so critical that she felt useless around them, or so needy that she felt drained by them. The worst part about her relationships, she claimed, was that she always picked men who were either impossibly out of her reach or impossibly beneath her. This often led to her being in a semi-committed relationship with a man who was safe and then having multiple affairs on the side with men who were dangerous. As she embraced more of the soul of adulthood, her esteem began to increase, her friendship patterns changed so that she felt mutually supported in her life, and she started dating men who actually had some long-term potential.

Having good self-esteem is part of being a strong, clear adult, but it is crucial to remember what we have outlined here. Self-esteem doesn't come in a pill. It is the result of messages we get about ourselves and of the competencies that we develop. If we want higher self-esteem, we need to risk being with people, and we need to work hard to develop our God-given talents. Affirmations are fine, but they are only a small fraction of this door to the soul of adulthood.

In closing this chapter, we want to offer one last tidbit of information that the reader might find useful. Adults who have high self-esteem don't talk about it in those terms, which supports in part what we have written here. They speak of the personal satisfaction of work well done, of the warmth and depth of friendships, of how much fun it is to learn to fly an airplane, of the challenge and excitment of changing jobs, and of how life isn't boring. But healthy adults rarely say, "Oh, I'm working on my self-esteem."

Chapter 9

THE DIGNITY OF LONELINESS

By all means use sometimes to be alone. Salute thyself; see what thy soul doth wear.

George Herbert
The Temple, 1633

The night is dark and still, so still that you can hear your heart beating slowly, forlornly, longing for an end to something. You are alone and your room is quiet; outside the air is motionless and inside it is heavy with your thoughts. You wonder if there is any pain worse than this loneliness that haunts you night after night, entering the room just after nightfall and prowling the edges of your dreams as you finally fall sleep in the early hours of the morning. It begins with an edgy feeling, a faceless restlessness that takes hold inside of you and begins to grow, becoming a dull ache in your chest before moving to the pit of your stomach, to the depths of your very soul, where it creates a void so vast it feels like it could contain the entire universe.

Sometimes as it approaches you act quickly, turning on the television, grabbing the newspaper or a dust rag, picking up the phone and dialing. Or you put on the shorts and t-shirt and the running shoes you bought last weekend and head out the door with the aim of doing your personal best on the five-mile course you laid out years ago. Better hurry, you tell yourself. That feeling is starting to take hold. A few more minutes and it will be so deeply embedded in your chest that you won't be able to run. Then you go. It wasn't your personal best, but the air was thick with the scent of jasmine and the moonlight cast its childlike spell across the soccer field. You thought you could hear the children's voices still rebounding off the trees, still echoing from yesterday's match. It is a loneliness you have felt before. As you enter your house, you wonder how long it will keep you up this night. It is a fickle ghost that haunts you.

At last you fall asleep and dream fitful dreams about disconnected pieces of self trying to find each other, of people you vaguely know—or do you?—trying to speak with silent voices. You awaken tired, and as the first rays of morning light appear the dull ache returns for a moment. You enter the new day with as much enthusiasm as you can muster in the hope that it will bring something new, some relief. The daytime is always easier. There is work, people with whom you can share ideas, tasks to be accomplished, places to go. You welcome the day because it is not the night. The loneliness subsides, at least until the moon shows its face on the darkened horizon. You wonder why God put the feeling of loneliness on the map of the human heart and what life would be like if we didn't feel it anymore.

SURVIVING IN TRIBES

Loneliness, or its corollary, fear of abandonment, is one of the most important experiences that human beings can have. The threat of permanent or unwanted separation from our fellow beings is so powerful that it has been used for thousands of years as a primary and effective form of punishment, whether it be solitary confinement in a maximum-security prison or a brief "time out" for an errant child. Chronic loneliness can even lead to premature death, a fact well established by gerontologists.

Every feeling is healthy, has an evolutionary survival function and conveys a message to us as well as others, if they are allowed to witness our feelings. Anger is crucial for our survival, as are shame, guilt, hurt, fear, joy, sadness and loneliness. Because we are essentially social animals, our very survival depends on us being connected to one another. We would not still exist on earth had we not organized ourselves into tribes. The earthly survival of complex beings like us depends upon the pooling of our individual resources—one is skilled at tracking prey, another at mediating disputes, a third at inventing new tools, a fourth at leading the rest in directions that assure future survival. Each person contributes his or her unique gifts and intelligences to the well-being of the group so that the group becomes more powerful and able to endure than any single individual.

THE IMPORTANCE OF SEPARATENESS

It would make sense to assume that we should want to dispense with aloneness altogether, that we were meant to be connected to one another and that separation from our fellows is inherently bad. But connection with others is only half of the picture; human beings also have a spiritual and biological drive to be separate. It is this ability that allows us to retain our uniqueness and to put our own special mark on the world. Alone in a laboratory a scientist seeks a cure for a deadly virus. Perhaps she works near others in her lab and indirectly with others through articles in medical journals, but there is something unique, something individualistic, that drives her to do her painstaking work each day. Much of her time is spent in solitude, her only companions being microscopic organisms, petri dishes, test tubes and a centrifuge.

A man pursues his dream of building a successful business, knowing that in the early years the only thing that will sustain the dream is his own motivation and will. If he is successful, people will join him in his success, but until then he will move it along through sheer determination and vision, in solitude. When others do swarm to join him, he will be faced with the dilemma of every successful entrepreneur, which is to carefully balance separateness and togetherness. If he loses his unique vision to the social pressures that now surround him, the business could lose its clarity and definition and be destroyed by the emerging competition. If he refuses to get help from others, he will be overwhelmed by the sheer size of what he is creating, and the business will sink. It is a marvel to observe someone like this as he keeps his vision and his power clear while enlisting the aid of an army of people who can help him turn the vision into reality.

Our separateness ensures that we are unique, that there is an individual person inside of us who is capable of being in relationship with others. This is why it is sad when we first begin therapy work with someone who came from a family where being a separate person was not encouraged, or worse, not allowed. We see men and women who are in the midst of a powerful and painful struggle that would have simply been a milestone were it not for the family messages they had received about separateness from the very beginning of life.

At approximately 18 months a child learns to say "no," which signals the beginnings of an internalized separate self. It is cause for celebration in healthy families because with it comes the promise of more independence, culminating in a young adult's emancipation from the family. Gradual separation from parents is what life is all about for a growing child, and as the child moves out into the world and takes her unique place in it, she experiences excitement and also the fear of being alone. How she learns to take care of her loneliness will play a major part in how far into adulthood she will be able to travel.

FIGHTING WITH OUR LONELINESS

Many years ago we began to tell our clients that they would be well on their way to healthy adulthood when they could choose to be lonely rather than to hurt someone, let someone hurt them or hurt themselves. While we are certain this statement is true, we are equally convinced that it is not an easy one to implement in our daily lives. Like all of human experience, loneliness has two sides to it, and one of them is very uncomfortable. We are not speaking here of the simple act of being alone. Learning to be alone, to appreciate one's solitude, is certainly essential to becoming an adult and is therefore a key factor in many conceptions of healthy adulthood such as Maslow's. But here we are referring to actual loneliness—the literal or figurative experience of being disconnected from our fellow beings, of being totally by ourselves, in isolation, abandoned.

Some people try to manage their loneliness with harmful diversions such as alcohol, food, dangerous hobbies or excessive activities such as exercising too much or working to exhaustion. While any one of these diversions may be healthy in moderaion, they can be very self-destructive if driven out of control by the pain of loneliness. When people finally try to set aside these distractions, it is often the pain of their loneliness that pushes them back toward the distraction. When a woman says that she has gone back to compulsive exercise because of a fight with her partner, what she really means is that she fears the relationship may be over—she fears abandonment.

Some people handle loneliness by hurting others. A man seduces one woman after another in the unconscious belief that each conquest will end the bitter loneliness deep inside of him. Or he tries to control a woman by physical force in the hope that he will possess her completely and therefore never be lonely again. In the name of loneliness, we manipulate, verbally assault, use guilt or shame, pout, threaten to withdraw our love entirely, scream and hit. We may cover our fear of loneliness with anger or intellectual argument, but we can't hide from it. All the anger in the world won't take away the pain of deep loneliness for very long.

Many people let themselves be hurt in the name of "loneliness-management." Sigmund Freud mistakenly wrote that women get into, or stay in, abusive relationships because of some peculiar need to be passive, dominated and controlled. In our experience, men and women don't leave abusive relationships, because they fear loneliness more than they fear abuse. For some people, it feels as if it is far better to be hurt regularly than to be lonely, because their past experiences with loneliness have been so limited and unhealthy. As Peter Charad said, "Until I came to terms with my own self and acquired some inner comfort, I did not have a choice of who I wanted to spend time with." That is why we say that you are well into adulthood if you can choose to be lonely rather than to let others hurt you.

THE DIGNITY OF LONELINESS

The depth of our dignity is tied closely to how we manage our loneliness, and it is our ability to make the best of our loneliness that signals our adulthood. In healthy families, children experience abandonment and loneliness in small doses so that over the years they learn how to cope with it, even gain from it. At two years, a child may cry hysterically when left with a babysitter, but if the sitter is good and his parents return as they said they would, eventually the child learns to trust that he can be separated from them and not die. It is the fear of death, after all, that lurks beneath the fear of abandonment.

That same child goes off to kindergarten when he is five years old and finds loneliness creeping in again, but if it is a good experience for him, he will learn that he can be separated from his parents and find substitutes in other people outside of his own home. He may feel lonely for awhile, but soon he learns to trust two things: that his parents will still be there at the end of the day, and that there are other trustworthy people in the world whose presence reduces feelings of loneliness. In other words, he learns that we are never alone if we are willing to reach out to others.

When he is a little older, he goes off to summer camp and the whole process begins all over again. Separation anxiety is followed by new discoveries. One evening while he and his fellow campers are sleeping under the stars, he looks up at the vast night sky and feels an overwhelming insignificance and loneliness. But it draws him in rather than pushing him away, and as he stares up at the stars, as he connects more and more with the void inside of himself that we all carry, he realizes that there is something good here, too. He maintains his focus, entranced by the interplay of vastness, loneliness, separation from his family and connectedness to his fellow campers. Finally, for one brief moment, he experiences a depth of peace with his own solitude that rivals the ineffable power and beauty of the very universe he has been contemplating.

It is a brief, and to some, an insignificantly subtle struggle that has just taken place inside this boy. But it is far from insignificant, because in addition to being able to choose loneliness over harm, life also challenges us to benefit from our loneliness. It is there for many purposes, one of which is to allow us to embrace ourselves at ever-deepening levels, which is what this boy did as he contemplated the loneliness, connectedness and infinite mystery of creation.

Inside each of us reside endless mazes of self-hood that are meant to be discovered over the deepening years of adulthood. If we are helped to experience our separation and loneliness in manageable doses as we grow up, we are then able to befriend our loneliness, to see it as an ally and not just as an uncomfortable feeling to be avoided. There is a unique dignity that is released and then courses through our souls when we are able to embrace our lone-liness. It is the embracing of self, the recognition and appreciation that we exist, that we matter, that we are.

In *The Search for the Real Self: Unmasking the Personality Disorders of Our Age,* a masterful work on bor-derline and narcissistic personality disorders, James Masterson writes that two of the most important aspects of being a healthy adult are the ability to soothe painful feel-ings and the ability to be alone. In many respects, fear of abandonment is the ultimate non-biological cause of most psychological disorders, from depression and anxiety attacks to personality disorders. Our universal fear of being cut off from one another, of being separated from our fel-low beings, is also an integral part of life, love and death. That is why one of the more powerful assignments that we can give to our clients is to go outside, sit under a tree with no radio, no journal, no friends, no dog—no distractions of any kind—and do nothing for at least an hour. When we give the assignment, people often look surprised, as if it will be so pointless or so easy that they wonder if we know what we're doing. When they return the next week, they have so much to report that it can take a whole session just to process what they felt, thought and discovered.

When our loneliness gets too big it is important to do something about it, whether that be calling a friend, see-ing a therapist or using a healthy distraction for awhile. But it is also important to recognize that if we are ever to enter adulthood there is a door that must be opened and through which we must pass. This door to adulthood can be a formidable one, offering resistances we never imag-ined possible. But it is one that each of us can open if we so choose. It lets us connect with our deeper selves, it lets us choose separation over abuse and self- destruction, and in the end, it allows us to live in harmony with life, love and death. The pain of loneliness can be incomprehensibly vast, and the depths of soul that are plumbed as we embrace our solitude can only be described as wondrous.

Chapter 10

TRADE-OFFS

My plenteous joys |Wanton in fullness, seek to hide themselves |In drops of sorrow

William Shakespeare
Macbeth, c. 1605

Adulthood is layered with wondrous intricacies that give it depth and meaning. It is much more than a simple extension of childhood. As we enter adolescence and begin struggling with personal identity, we are faced with a dizzying array of choices that include career, values, beliefs, lifestyle, religion and sexuality. As society becomes increasingly complex, many people lament the passing of simpler times in which a son learned his father's trade and a daughter's only option was to marry and bear children. While there were certainly divorces in days gone by, the ease of entering into and ending marital commitments has increased dramatically.

It is as if the number of buttons and knobs on the remote control devices in our living rooms is a direct reflection of the number of choices now available to us. And like our response to many of those buttons and knobs, we look at everything laid out before us on life's table and simply shudder in a spasm of confused paralysis. It seems as if there are too many choices and not enough years in a lifetime to sample them all.

And yet many of us open the door to adulthood and go about our lives despite this proliferation of life possibilities. For some of us, the question is, "How?" How does a young man or woman make the transition into adulthood in the face of so many choices? Some of the critical pieces in this puzzle are the adult abilities to experiment with life, to experience possibilities, to evaluate what has been learned, to test those choices against some internal template of feeling and meaning, and to then begin narrowing the options.

It stands to reason that to accomplish this complicated sorting and selection an adult must have at least three components of soul upon which to draw. She must have a basic core self from which her life sampling can be evaluated, she must be willing to take risks so that she can try new things, and she must have fairly clear internal limits so that she can choose to turn down one positive or negative option in the face of another positive or negative option. In other words, if she is faced with a choice of three flavors of ice cream, each of which she likes equally, she'll be paralyzed unless she can pick one and release the other two for the time being, and maybe forever.

Accepting trade-offs is an unquestionably essential part of growing up. A young man must either accept his third choice to attend an excellent state university on a partial scholarship, or his first choice, a private university but with no scholarship. A young woman must choose to accept her first professional job with a firm that has better salary and benefits but fewer women in senior management, or a firm that has more women in senior management but less attractive financial compensation. A young couple must decide whether to move to a big city where rents are higher but career options are greater, or to stay in a small town where job opportunities are limited but the cost of living is lower. More and more people struggle with the questions of if or when to have children, if or when to get married, if or when to make that last big career move, and if, when, or where to retire. It is no wonder we feel dizzy sometimes.

A core self, risk taking and internal limits are not aspects of soul that just appear when we enter puberty. They evolve out of the rich earth that is family, beginning in infancy and growing throughout adulthood. So when a man says that he had a marvelous childhood with no shortages anywhere at all, but that he has been paralyzed and stuck in his life for years, it is significant. It is the prologue to his story, not the conclusion, and a few simple questions often help to loosen the soil. We might ask, "What do you like about life? What fires your spirit and brings you passion?" If he doesn't know or is vague and confused, it might indicate a shortage in his core self. We might ask, "Have you had other job experiences over the years?" If he says that his job history is limited, it might tell us something about risk. It might be a core self, risk and internal limits issue if he says, "I really love sales and personnel work equally, and because I can't pick one or the other, I stay with this third alternative that I hate, but I don't know why."

Accepting trade-offs is inseparable from questions of entitlement, disappointment, struggle and resistance. A woman who believes she is entitled to anything that her impulses dictate will be in a constant state of unease punctuated by disappointment, anger and feelings of victimization. Life will always seem harsh and unfair. She will view the people in her life as intentionally punishing—on earth to make her miserable—and she will lash out in self-protection. This just pushes people away from her, leaving her in isolation and despair. It is especially sad because each of us is so close to this particular door to adulthood.

If we think of this woman's dilemma as a stone, then she doesn't need to flip it over and or smash it and examine the fragments under a microscope. She has already tried that, and the harder she tries the more frustrated and bitter she becomes. She would only have to rotate the stone a few degrees in either direction, and the answer would be there in front of her, simply and elegantly. To begin living more peacefully in adulthood, all she would need to say is, "Life will permit me to have some of the things I want, but not all of them."

TRADE-OFFS IN FAMILIES

The value of learning to accept trade-offs is especially poignant when we work with family members in conflict. A man worked very hard to make sense of his self-destructive behavior and in the process identified some painful aspects of his childhood. He understood that to simply blame his parents for his current problems would be too shallow, leaving him in a victim state with no responsibility for his own life. And he knew that to ignore his childhood pain would be unrealistic, leaving him with unhealed shame. He decided that one way to achieve some balance between the two would be to share parts of his discoveries with his parents in the hope that they would acknowledge that some things in his childhood were less than ideal. He invited them into a therapy session and they agreed to attend. With high hopes for a major breakthrough, the man began to share some of his early pain with them, only to find that they had a hard time just listening. They hadn't done the work that he had, and so with the best of intentions, they tried to explain why they had done what they had done each time he brought up an issue. It was clear that they were trying, but it was also evident that he would not achieve the simple, deep recognition that he sought. At his next individual session, the man was hurt and confused. He asked, "What do I do now?"

As we worked with his disappointment, he began to formulate his own answer to the question. Over the succeeding months he grew to realize that he had some choices and that it was up to him to pick one of them. At first he chose to be bitter and angry, distancing himself from his parents in the hopes that they would feel the pain of his rejecting them and thereby see how they had rejected him. But they just weren't getting it. He would talk to them occasionally, but they always seemed confused. They wanted to help, they told him, but they just didn't understand what he wanted. He gradually let go of this choice, and as he did, this door to adulthood slowly opened. A few months later he came in and announced that he had decided to accept them for who they were, and to get what he could from them rather than trying to get what he couldn't. The door opened wide as tears of grief and dignity trickled down his cheeks. He had chosen to trade a fantasy of what could be for what was real and possible—to have a limited relationship with his parents rather than none at all. By doing so, he retrieved his power from the tight grip of his past, allowing him to live his life more fully.

MAJOR TRADE-OFFS IN ADULTHOOD

It may not always be obvious, but whenever we move from one stage of our lives into the next, something is lost, and the very loss that is so painful opens the door to the promise of what will be gained. This is an inherent feature of a tradeoff. We grow attached to a rusty old car but its unreliability becomes a hazard. With reluctance, we trade it in for a new car that lacks the character and uniqueness of the one that has grown on us. And it takes months before we grow into the new one, becoming familiar with its quirks and creating a sense of personal ownership like we had with the old one. It is hard to admit at first that the new car is safer and more reliable. Eventually it grows on us and we can relish the fact that we don't have to worry if it will start every morning, and that we have a much better chance of surviving an accident than in the old one.

Couples who have created a deep, abiding, long-term love for one another know the importance of trade-offs more than most. Over the years they carve out large spaces in their souls to accommodate the quirks and idiosyncrasies of their partner, knowing that there is no such thing as a mate who fulfills all of one's fantasies. She accompanies him to an action movie on occasion because he enjoys them and she appreciates his company, even though she could do without the movie. He watches a sentimental movie with her for the same reason. They give up something and get something in return, but without keeping score. He puts the toilet seat down because it's important to her despite the reverse logic that would suggest she put it up for him. She ignores his dirty running shorts hanging in the bathroom, unless they're really grungy. And at various times when they fight, one or the other can give in simply because their partner is feeling down and just needs to be heard.

LIFE TRADE-OFFS

We don't have to wait for a job or marital dilemma to arise before we can be invited through this door to adulthood. Life itself offers us plenty of opportunities to choose alternatives and accept trade-offs. As our biological clocks keep ticking we are confronted with the choice to have children or not, to continue growing up or not, to let go of our children when they reach adulthood or not, and to age gracefully or not. For many years we have likened the household with teenagers to an airport, with the parents on the main runway checking their equipment to see if they are ready to take off or not, and the young adults stacked up behind them on the taxiway waiting to get out on the main runway. Human development doesn't stop at age 21. Adults have stages that they can go through, too, if they choose.

With consummate wisdom, Erik Erikson wrote that "Healthy children will not fear life, if their parents have integrity enough not to fear death." To Erikson, integrity meant the sense of wholeness and completion about one's self and one's life that can only come from facing each stage of adulthood with courage and openness. Consistent with his theorizing, adults who have faced life's crises head on do not fear death. They elegantly view death as yet another stage of life, and having faced the other stages, they welcome the challenge. When parents have with children about to leave the nest, the challenge is to head down the runway at full speed and fly into the next stage of life, freeing their young adults to move from the taxiway out onto the main runway. In certain families, the parents are somehow stuck, afraid of what will happen when they no longer have children dependent upon them. Some parents fear that their marriage will not hold up without the distraction, while others are caught in a struggle to acknowledge their own mortality. In those families, the young adults stack up on the taxiway one behind the other, agitated, tense, too comfortable but at some level knowing it. It is as if an unspoken bargain has been struck—"You kids stay little so that we don't have to grow up anymore. We'll be sure to fuel your tanks every so often so that you won't have to learn to do it yourselves, and so that it looks as if you're about to go even though you aren't.

Developmental theorist Robert Peck expanded Erikson's adult stages to include a number of adjustments or trade-offs we face in adulthood. Two of these that have a bearing on the emptying of the nest are Cathectic Flexibility vs. Cathectic Impoverishment and Mental Flexibility vs. Mental Rigidity. Cathexis has to do with our emotional attachments to people and things, and so this first tradeoff includes the struggle to let go of old attachments and embrace new ones, which is a crucial factor in getting the whole family into the empty nest phase of life. Young adults need to see their parents embracing new activities and a new lifestyle because it releases the children from the burden of rescuing their parents, and because it shows young adults how to grow old gracefully themselves. Because Cathectic Impoverishment sounds so negative you might wonder where the current tradeoff is, but if you think about it, letting go of longstanding emotional investments can be frightening. Hanging onto the known is often more attractive than moving forward, which is why some in middle age unconsciously keep their young adults in the nest by financing their lives or by trying to control them in ways no longer appropriate. The underlying message is, "I fear growing, I fear living and I fear death, so stay back on the taxiway and give me a good reason to stay right where I am."

Another tradeoff facing every person who makes it into middle age or beyond is connected to our inevitable physical decline. Peck described this as the adjustment of Valuing Wisdom vs. Valuing Physical Powers. Some adults move into middle age with such grace and dignity that it is a wonder to behold, while others fight with the aging process so strenuously that we wonder what dark force is controlling them. Like a man trying to stop a tornado from hitting his house by angrily shaking his fist, some people feel bitter and frightened by their physical decline. They don't just exercise because it's good for their health, they exercise with an insane intensity that says, "If you stop, you'll die!" Or they become depressed, withdrawn and preoccupied with their bodies, leaving little psychological energy left for anything else.

People who can make the shift to Valuing Wisdom open a door to a life that couldn't have existed at a younger age. Wisdom is the result of living a full life. It brings knowledge and decision-making abilities that can't be taught in the classroom, and it allows people to accomplish more and have more healthy power despite aching muscles and weakening eyesight. A wise business executive doesn't relinquish her power within the corporation because she is getting physically weaker, she simply magnifies her power and uses it to accomplish her goals by rallying younger people behind her unique corporate vision. A wise teacher has worked in the field so long that he can easily become more creative in his methods if he chooses, and he has the time to develop new leadership abilities that can keep him at the top of his field well past his so-called prime.

Facing this tradeoff requires facing the inevitability of one's mortality because few things remind us of it more acutely than physical decline. But once we trade this desperate fear of death with the embracing of powers that can only come with age, we enter an adulthood filled with life, love, challenge, excitement, risk, accomplishment, success and emotional depth that wasn't possible before. It is exciting to grow older, and as we do it gracefully we help to open up the earlier doors through which we have passed so that our children can grow up too.

Chapter 11

NARCISSISM

Selfishness is not living as one wishes to live. It is asking others to live as one wishes to live.

Oscar Wilde
The Soul of Man Under Socialism, 1891

It is good to feel special now and then. Whether it be due to a unique accomplishment or a unique trauma, there are times when any human being needs to feel special, i.e., separate and apart from all other human beings, because it affirms our identity, our very existence. But like everything else in this book, if separateness starts to push out toward the extremes, it then becomes pathological. Each one of us is unique and special, but we are also more similar to each other than some of us would like to admit. The question is: "How special must we try to be before it becomes unhealthy?"

A great deal has been written about narcissism since the 1960s, from Christopher Lasch's *The Culture of Narcissism* to parts of Thomas Moore's *Care of the Soul.* One of the better clinical descriptions of narcissistic personality disorder was written by James Masterson in *The Search for the Real Self: Unmasking the Personality Disorders of Our Age.* We have already written quite a bit about narcissism in the present book because disappointment, entitlement, lack of identity and loss of self, among others, are all features of the narcissism with which each of us must struggle. Because the term has such negative connotations, many people do not like to read that all adults must struggle with narcissism. When we hear the word, we think of someone who is selfish, self-absorbed, shallow, empty, knows it all, is interested only in externals and appearances—a person who is so taken with himself that nothing else in the universe is very important to him. In truth, how much these traits describe an individual is more a matter of degree than all-or-none.

It is part of our normal narcissism when we identify with Abraham Lincoln or Mary Magdalene and then briefly believe that we are as powerful, wise, altruistic or courageous as them. And then reality sets in and we discover that our limitations are greater than we had fantasized. Our narcissism operates when we are so enthused about something that we don't give others a tactful way to enter the conversation, or when we put down their contributions as trite. It is present when we become overly defensive in the face of appropriate criticism from others. It is present when we apply to ourselves everything that others talk about rather than listening empathetically, such as the man who always says, "Oh, that happened to me! When it happened to me, I did this and I did that." He always seems to cut others off in mid-sentence so that what was meant to be the other person's turn to talk quickly becomes his turn to talk—again and again. And narcissism is present when we assume that everyone else feels or thinks the same way that we do.

DIAGNOSTIC CRITERIA

When one's narcissism becomes extreme, it is then cat-egorized as an emotional disorder. The *Diagostic and Statistical Manual* of the American Psychiatric Association (DSM-IV) defines Narcissistic Personality Disorder as "A pervasive pattern of grandiosity (in fantasy or behavior), need for admiration and lack of empathy" as typified by grandiosity; fantasies of unlimited success, power, bril-liance, beauty or love; feeling "special" and therefore need-ing to associate only with other "special" people and institutions; needing excessive admiration; a distorted sense of entitlement; being exploitive of others; lacking empathy; being envious of others or believing that others are envious of you; and displaying arrogant behaviors or attitudes.

Masterson observed with detached amusement that his office was flooded with phone calls from people seeking therapy with him after they saw him quoted in *The New York Times*. Because they saw him as a national expert, and because they had to work with "the best" in the country, once their evaluations had been completed and they were told they would have to work with one of Masterson's asso-ciates, they never returned. People with this disorder are similar to those with borderline personality disorder in that their inner core, or real self as Carl Rogers called it, is empty, undeveloped, unformed, malnourished from infancy, a ver-itable vacuum. The difference is that for the narcissist, his or her outer shell of defenses and coping mechanisms—what Masterson called the false self—is generally more effective than the borderline's, exceptions always noted, of course. This empty core self explains all of the diagnostic symptoms and behavior patterns listed above.

THE FINANCIALLY SUCCESSFUL NARCISSIST

Lacking the depth of soul that true adults have, the narcissist is in constant need of praise and adoration in attempts to fuel the complex external shield of the false self that he has constructed. One way to create this fantasy is to be special. A financially successful narcissist seems to do just fine as long as he can surround himself with people who will adore him and fawn over him. His financial success fuels the external shield with expensive cars, extravagant houses and grand vacations to the four corners of the globe. His successful facade can work in the business world where deeper intimacy does not need to be part of the game. It is in the world of intimate relationships where the narcissist's problems stand out most clearly.

Struggling but unable to acknowledge his own shortcomings, and therefore unable to acknowledge his own shame, the narcissist is too internally fragile to handle the complex reciprocity that is required in intimacy. He may dump his own shame onto those around him, and lacking empathy, he has no idea why some people later become furious with him for doing it. For example, a man was always doing things that he termed "very important," and as a result, he was always letting down those around him. He was constantly late for dates and appointments, he neglected friendships, he used other people for his own ends and truly believed that he was so special that others would not mind stepping aside for him.

When his own ten-year-old daughter finally shared with him how hurt she was that he was always one to two hours late to pick her up for their visits, he turned it around and made it about her. He told her that she was too sensitive and that he didn't do it on purpose anyway, it was just that he had some "very important" things to do. He even contacted his ex-wife and began to blame her for his daughter's negative feelings towards him. As a child, his daughter believed there was something wrong with her. As she grew older, she realized that her father was damaged and empty inside, and then she just felt sorry for him despite his success in business.

Of course, there are successful people who have wonderful relationships and who do not use their material possessions as part of an elaborate unconscious facade. The difference is that their relationship to their own accomplishments and to their loved ones is realistic, open and balanced. Healthy people are emotionally available and accessible in ways that are simply not possible for the narcissist. At the same time, there are plenty of narcissistic people who never succeed in their careers because of their grandiosity and lack of empathy. They tend to start things with a grand flourish and are able to generate lots of enthusiasm from others at the outset because they look so good on the outside. However their inability to follow through with commitments, along with their honest belief that they are more special than their associates, often dooms their ultimate success. And so they go through life viewing the expensive cars and homes not as pleasant by-products of a successful career, but as ends in themselves.

RELIGIOSITY AND NARCISSISM

There are other manifestations of this personality disorder in our culture. The feelings of being "special" and "different" show themselves in the grandiosity of the religiously manipulative person who actually believes that he has a unique direct pipeline to God. Unlike a truly spiritual person, the narcissist will capitalize on his seductive abilities to control others, inevitably exploiting them. In response to his own sexual acting out, macabre religious caricature Jimmy Swaggert sobbed on national television. A few years later when he was discovered to be acting out sexually again, he informed us that God told him to tell the rest of us to shut up. Oral Roberts claimed that God told him that He would take Oral up to heaven if people didn't contribute enough money to Oral's enterprises; fortunately people came through and Oral was spared an untimely death. A few years later, realizing that it does not make good marketing sense to use God's name twice in the same way, he claimed that God said Oral would go to hell unless we gave him eight million dollars more.

Contrast those words and actions with those of Mother Theresa who, when asked by reporters what it was like to be a living saint, said:

> You have to be holy in your position, as you are. And I have to be holy in the position that God has put me. So it is nothing extraordinary to be holy. Holiness is not the luxury of the few. Holiness is a simple duty for you and for me. We have been created for that.

The narcissistic parent or religious figure may sincerely believe his deluded fantasies of special spiritual powers, but adults who have reached down into the depths of their souls can usually detect the false humility and obvious grandiosity of claims such as those of Swaggert or Roberts. At the same time, those healthy adults will immediately resonate to the powerful, simple humility of a Mother Theresa. She is a spiritual leader in part because she neither states nor implies that she has a special pipeline to God.

ADOLESCENCE, VICTIMHOOD AND NARCISSISM

Piagetian psychologist David Elkind wrote a great deal about the cognitive changes that happen during normal adolescence. As a result of the emerging mental maturity that occurs during this period in our lives, an adolescent will develop distortions in thinking and perceiving that explain some of his perplexing behavior. Elkind named two of these distortions the "personal fable" and the "imaginary audience." The former includes the adolescent's belief in his own immortality, which explains some of the foolish risks that many adolescents take. It also refers to his belief that he is so unique that no one could ever understand him. He might say to his parents, "I appreciate your attempts to understand how I'm feeling about breaking up with Julie, but this love that I just lost was so unique, so deep and so special that there is no way you can grasp what it is like for me." As he experiences more of life and shares it with others, he realizes that others feel the same deep pain when losing a first love, which means he is not as special as he first thought. The tradeoff is that he loses some of his feelings of being special while he gains the comfort of knowing that he is not alone in the universe. He also gains the emotional depth that comes with being an adult.

The imaginary audience refers to the adolescent's belief and feeling that he is on stage—that he is so special that he stands out, and everyone is watching him and noticing every little detail and flaw. This explains why many adolescents spend so much time in front of the mirror and why they are so self-conscious. In a high school speech class, it would be typical for each student to believe that the other students are on the edge of their seats just waiting for some major piece of brilliance to applaud, or for some major faux pas to occur so that they can laugh at him. In truth, some of the students may be listening and watching intently, but many of them may actually be thinking about their own speeches and worrying how they will do when it is their turn. Again, as the adolescent shares his experiences and inner feelings with his peers, he begins to get a realistic picture of how "un-special" he really is, which is both a disappointment and a relief.

Erik Erikson described our personality development as an ever-expanding view of mankind that begins with the total egocentrism of the newborn infant who cannot distinguish himself from his caretakers, to the broad wisdom of an old person who appreciates his connection with all of humanity in the past, present and future. The depth and breadth of an aged person's connectedness with creation is wondrous to behold, and it can only emerge if he is gradually willing to let go of his narcissism in stages all the way along life's path.

For the adolescent, the challenge is to gradually let go of beliefs that support the "personal fable" and the "imaginary audience." He talks to his friends after the speech class is over and discovers that many of them were concentrating on their own speeches. He contracts a minor sexually transmitted disease and realizes that he must think about his own safety in the future if he wants to stay alive. He talks to people about how he looks and finds out that nobody even noticed the small pimple on his face that he thought was the size of Mount Everest. He learns that while his pain is real, it isn't any more painful than that of other human beings in the same circumstances.

If an adolescent has significant emotional shortages from a painful childhood, it will be difficult for him to release these narcissistic beliefs. As he moves into his twenties and thirties, he may get stuck in his own victimhood and focus intently and exclusively on the depth of his own pain. He may become totally absorbed in that pain and then build the victim filter that causes him to perceive the world as a constant threat. And in his self-absorption, he may begin to push people away by talking incessantly about his problems. For many years we have said in our lectures that there is only one person on earth who is as interested as you are in your own personal story and your own personal pain. That person is you. Our parents will be interested in our pain to some degree, our siblings may be interested to some degree, and certainly our lover will be interested to some degree. But the narcissist believes that everyone is, or at least should be, as interested in her pain as she is. And thus she corners people at family get-togethers or at parties and begins a painfully tedious monologue of her recent physical or emotional sorrows, offering plenty of details so that you can appreciate her tragedies as fully as she does.

The narcissism of victimhood also appears when we try to make people indebted to us by doing things for them. We tell ourselves that we bend over backwards to help all those around us simply because we are kind, generous and altruistic. But then we become unconsciously hurt and angry at others if they don't return all of our favors. We become morally righteous and superior as we remind people of "all we've done for them." We seem to forget the definition of "gift," which means something that is freely given, with no expectation for repayment and no strings attached. The owe/pay syndrome as we called it in our first book, derives from the child's noble attempts to get his needs met in an unhealthy family, and it is one of the more destructive patterns in adult relationships.

BEYOND NARCISSISM

A common narcissistic pattern is to find a hero or new love to idealize and then almost immediately begin to look for their flaws until we are disappointed, disillusioned and angry. This pattern typifies the extreme thought process of most personality disorders and many other emotional problems, in which life is black-and-white, all-or-none. A good way to begin moving beyond one's narcissism is to think more moderately—to start looking at the shades of gray between black and white. As she struggles with a new partner, a woman might say to herself, "I thought he was perfect and now I am finding out that he isn't. I feel like hurting him for disappointing me, but he didn't do anything. It was unrealistic for me to expect perfection. What can I appreciate about him? And how can I deepen by accepting his flaws?" When referring to how much some of us berate ourselves amidst our own pain, John Holtzermann asks, "On what authority are you making this judgment about yourself?" When we can accept our own flaws graciously, it is easier to accept the flaws of others.

To move beyond these many forms of narcissism requires what may sound like contradictory advice. We need to share our pain with others so that we can heal our wounds, but we also need to learn to recognize when others have had enough. When we risk sharing with people who are healthy, they will let us know these limits in a firm but gracious manner. When we share with people who are not so healthy, they will rarely let us know, and so we won't learn anything from the relationship. When a healthy person resists our manipulations, we may feel shame and rage. If we want to grow up, we need to accept our share of the responsibility for that shame and rage and let it deepen us.

We must also learn to create balance in our relationships so that when we give of ourselves we can do it freely. There is nothing wrong with consciously putting our personal needs aside for the betterment of others as long as we know we're doing it, as long as we're choosing it freely and as long as we can maintain balance between self-care and care of others. Indeed, we are all unique and special, and we have a right and a responsibility to celebrate that. But we are also part of a much greater universe of other human beings who are very much like us. To maintain our uniqueness while acknowledging that we are but a tiny part of creation is one of the many joys that come when we pass through this door to the soul of adulthood.

Chapter 12

VICTIMHOOD

Ask not what your country can do for you. Ask what you can do for your country.

John F. Kennedy

While each of us grapples with layers of meaning inside of us, there are also parallel struggles going on in the broader world outside. The two are obviously related because our political and historical dramas are reflections of the myriad layers of our individual longings as they emerge, express themselves and collide with one another. Whatever is in our hearts gets projected out onto our leaders, and conversely, our leaders find themselves in power at least in part because they have found a way to resonate with our longings. So when John F. Kennedy gave his electrifying inaugural address in 1961, he put some of us in a bind. A new leader carries into power all of the hopes, dreams and anxieties of the people whom he leads, and many people have high hopes that their new leader will do something for them to make their lives better. But there he was telling us not how he was going to improve America, but how we could improve America by taking responsibility for it ourselves.

It was a brilliantly hypnotic remark and many of us responded, carried along by our enchantment with his public image. Kennedy was energetic, sophisticated, charming, detached and intellectual, and thus tapped directly into the spirit of an America ready for the new era of media-dominated politics. As there are many layers to the soul of an individual, nations have many-layered souls, too. At one level it didn't matter if he was a womanizer or if his physical health was bad, because we didn't want or need to know these things about him at the time. It would have hurt too much to know. We were not only in an age of cold war, détente and space races, but also an age of innocence and naiveté, at least on the conscious plane.

As we get ready to enter the 21st century, many feel that our country has gone to hell in a handbasket, and at a very superficial level that may be true. The world seems darker, more complicated and more anxiety-ridden today than it did in the early 1960s. Over the past 30 years, there have been countless dialectical struggles over civil rights, economics, communism versus capitalism, women's rights, rights of the poor and homeless, and many others. We have battled in Congress, in the streets, in our bedrooms and boardrooms, and some would say that all we have to show for it is a high divorce rate and a lot of latchkey children waiting at home for their single parent to return from work at the end of a long day.

But that gloomily oversimplified analysis is probably just as inaccurate as was our naiveté in the 1960s—things are different, not necessarily worse. Each generation appears to have its particular struggles that must be played out. Today, some social critics suggest that we are engaged in a national struggle between victim and perpetrator. We have analyzed these concepts back and forth on television talk shows for so many years now we seem to be spinning inside a maelstrom of confused finger-pointing. Who can tell the good guys from the bad guys anymore? Everything has become so muddy and relative that murderers go free because juries feel sorry for them, and people don't know if their memories are real, imagined or simply there by a therapist's suggestion. We seem to have lost both our moral compass and our sense of personal accountability.

Charles Sykes makes a compelling case for his belief that we have steered a course into the treacherous waters of victimism—a mindset in which each of us sees himself as a victim of someone else's offenses. Rather than accepting that life doesn't always work out the way we would like, we now file lawsuits as easily as we change disposable razors. If we are unhappy, then somebody else must be to blame. After all, this is America the land of entitlement, in which we now only ask what our country can do for us. If Sykes' thesis is correct, then it follows that no matter what the real cause of our misery may be, there must be someone who can be made to pay for it.

We suspect that Sykes' book may be reviled by many people who only see centuries of social injustice needing to be rectified. However, he asserts quite strongly that victims of abuse and neglect have every right to be respected for their victim status and to get the help that they need to move beyond it. The emotions surrounding victimization in America appear so powerful, so unconscious and so deep that many people don't hear that part of his message. They hear the word "victimism" and become outraged. But as psychologists who work daily with victims of childhood trauma, we cannot ignore the fact that when victimhood becomes institutionalized, victims have little choice but to remain victims. Over the years, we have learned a very difficult truth—that if one is to stop being victimized in the future he must first face the fact of his victimhood, work through the pain of the trauma, and then take responsibility for his life in the present. In simpler terms, he must first heal the old wounds and then learn how to become an adult.

INSIDE THE VICTIM ROLE

As annoying as the debate about political correctness may sometimes be, it isn't trivial. Words are one of our primary tools to maintain connection with each other, and they are in constant social evolution. In the 1950s it was Freudian-chic to know that human beings react strongly to the word "mother." Mothers are so important in our early development that no matter what kind of relationship we have with them our reactions will be marked. The word "death" has similar emotional richness for many, as do the words "earthquake" and "tornado." Words are symbols for ideas, events, things and feelings that have meaning for us, great or small; lately, the word "victim" has gained considerable emotional power in American society.

A woman we knew believed that if she admitted she was a victim of something she would dissolve into a puddle of shame. This reaction to the word often signals our fear of admitting our limitations, which is a formidable limitation in itself. At the other extreme is a man who believed that unless society legally acknowledged his victimhood by requiring payment of some sort, he would be trapped in it for all eternity, never to be happy or fulfilled, which is also a formidable trap in itself. The simple truth is that neither stance is particularly balanced or helpful. After all, each of us has been a victim of something. When a fire destroys a house and most of the owner's possessions it threatens his trust in the world. When a parent dies suddenly in a traffic accident, a child's world is turned upside down. Uncertainty and tragedy are part of life, and healthy adults acknowledge and accept these inevitable dangers as part of the challenge of living.

To deny victimization can be as dangerous as it is to embrace victimhood as a lifestyle. An earthquake survivor might say, "I'm not going to be a victim about it. I had insurance. I'll rebuild. My neighbor is the one who really needs help. What can you do for her?" Is he saying that the earthquake didn't scare him? That he hasn't been traumatized by it? That he hasn't suffered a profound loss? While his words say one thing we may assume at another level that he must be in shock, or that he must be ashamed of his vulnerability or that he has never learned to attach words to his feelings. Loss is a universally painful experience. Some people hear the word "victim" and then quickly begin to build up a verbal defense against it. "I'm in a pretty tricky relationship, but don't get me wrong. I'm not a victim," one might say. "At work I'm strong and successful. I just have to figure out this relationship and then everything will be okay." Another might say, "I'm not one of those whiney victims. I've always been in control of my own destiny. I take responsibility for my life. My boss isn't abusive. She's just competitive."

It may not be a surprise to hear this, but most people who are trapped in the victim role are unaware of it. St. Paul psychologists James Maddock and Noel Larson explain that a person who is living inside of the victim role actually has a filter through which all experiences are interpreted from the stance of victimization. A therapist might say, "I think you have a lot of untapped resources and strengths," and the client will filter it into, "This therapist is really telling me that I'm not doing my life good enough." A woman's plane is delayed and there is nothing that the ticket agent can do, but the victim sees this as a personal affront, saying to the agent, "You know damned well that you could do something to help me out here. If I were wealthy or famous, you'd get that plane here on time for me!" Or a man declines an offer to join his associate for dinner because he has a previous commitment; and the associate, who is responding from inside his victim role, accuses the man of declining out of dislike for him. Confused by all of this pouting and posturing, the man may now be more guarded when approached by this associate in the future. This will reinforce the associate's distorted belief that this man doesn't like him.

Living life from the stance of a victim has limits at the very least, and at the worst, it can be dangerously life-threatening. Looking out upon the world from inside the victim role, the world can look like a dark and foreboding place that is inhabited primarily by perpetrators, offenders, fair-weather friends, manipulators and con-artists. This victim filter makes the world seem so awful that the only sane response in many cases is to be chronically depressed or chronically angry, as if the world were one huge prison cell from which the victim is serving out a life sentence without the possibility of parole.

In trying to get out of this metaphorical prison of victimism, it is sometimes helpful to focus for awhile on the composition of the walls, bars, doors and windows of the prison that keep the victim from entering the free world of adulthood. With that knowledge, a victim might be more likely to find a door into a better life. When we look out at the world through those bars, what are they made of? Are they composed of a belief system that says, "Nothing good ever happens?" Are they embedded in concrete walls that say, "No one cares" or "I will never be happy?" If these are our guiding life principles, then we will be caught in a prison more real than San Quentin.

Over the years we have observed certain beliefs, feelings and behaviors that make up the victim role. People who are caught in this painful place may not recognize themselves at first in the following paragraphs, which is why it is important to know that we all do these things now and then. In the case of victimism, these things become part of a lifestyle rather than an occasional occurrence.

With victimism comes a deeply felt sense of one's helplessness and powerlessness which leads one to wait for what he wants or needs, to wait for others to change, to wait for life to get better. What looks like patience to some is actually a set of beliefs, feelings and behaviors that are screaming out from the depths, "There is something I deserve or need, but the only way I'll get it is if someone else reads my mind and then chooses to give it to me. I don't have the power to make it happen for myself." If you were to challenge such thinking, you would encounter impenetrable resistance from the victim in the form of very rational arguments. A man might say, "I can't do anything about this horrible situation at work because my boss is an impossible jerk and I've put in for a transfer but there aren't any openings right now." Or a woman might say, "My partner keeps making nasty remarks to me in public, but there's nothing I can do. I've asked him to stop hundreds of times but it just doesn't do any good. He doesn't listen to me."

With victimism it is always somebody else's fault. People who have embraced their victimhood blame everyone else for their problems and take very little responsibility for their lives, as if interactions between adults were 100 percent-0 percent rather than fifty-fifty. A man whose wife is alcoholic says that his misery is due entirely to her addiction. A woman whose children won't help around the house blames it wholly on her spouse. In each case, the victim truly believes that he has no power to change and no responsibility for his life, as if he is a very young child whose parents must still make most day-to-day decisions for him.

Victimism also includes the belief that we don't have choices, which leads to a deep spiritual, emotional and behavioral paralysis. Even a prisoner in an eight-by-eight cell has choices every day, but in our victimism we surrender those choices for the safety of remaining unaccountable and emotionally little. Again, if you were to ask the victim if he would like things to be different he would assert vociferously that it is all he dreams about. He might even get angry at you for implying that he wants to remain paralyzed in his life. But when you look at his behavior, beyond his protests, all you can see is a person who is choosing to stay put for some reason.

This surrender of choice is especially evident in cases of chronic pain, chronic illness or addiction, and it is understandable in these cases. Of course the man with chronic leg pain from an automobile accident caused by a drunk driver would like to have the pain disappear, and of course he is initially justified in his rage and blame at the person who drove while drunk. We can sympathize with his plight and would prefer it to be different for him, but if he is ever to have a life again he must eventually focus on the available alternatives, not unavailable ones. To sit around and wish that the pain would be gone won't help; to learn what he can do to manage the pain and become a player in life, will.

To acknowledge our victimism—our paralysis based on feelings and beliefs of powerlessness—is a formidable task. It is painful, embarrassing and scary to leave the miserable safety of victimism, because for many it has become a way of life. But for many it can become a former way of life. A woman we know told us that she had listened to John Kennedy's inaugural address again and had decided to remove "If only . . ." and "But . . ." from her vocabulary when she spoke of difficulties in her life. With that simple realization, she was ready to acknowledge her victimhood and take her first shaky steps into the soul of adulthood.

Chapter 13

BEYOND DYSFUNCTIONAL ROLES

He that will not command his thoughts . . . will soon lose the command of his actions.

Thomas Wilson
Sacra Privata, c. 1755

In *Becoming Partners: Marriage and Its Alternatives,* Carl Rogers described four threads that he believed run throughout all healthy relationships. He strongly felt that one of these threads is the importance of moving beyond stereotyped roles, because rigidity in any system eventually causes problems. If Dad is the only one to handle the finances and then Dad dies, the rest of the family is in serious trouble for awhile. If Mom is the only one to wash clothes or prepare meals and she goes on vacation by herself, then the family will experience great stress. Having clear roles in life is just fine—it's the rigid and stereotyped ones that lead to trouble. To truly embrace adulthood, we must both identify the dysfunctional roles in which we may be stuck and then begin to move away from them.

SYSTEMS, NEEDS AND ROLES

A family is a system that like all systems in nature has both a purpose for its existence and a structure to help fulfill that purpose. As Abraham Maslow and many family-systems theorists have noted, families exist for the survival and growth of the individuals in them as well as for the continuation of our species. When we consider all of its nuances and implications, this observation is quite startling, and it helps to explain much of human behavior.

Human needs are very complex and the variety of ways that we can meet our needs is endless. We can't thrive on just the basic biological sustenance of food and water. We need to love and be loved, we need to be valued and have worth, we need to be alone at times, we need to know and discover, we need complex stimulation, we need to be challenged, we need to play and we need to be spiritual. And because no system is without error, every family system needs to make room for mistakes and to learn from them and correct them without too much damage accruing in the system. In a healthy system, each family member gets each of these needs met on a fairly regular basis and in fairly regular doses. Every person in the family must be valued and prized, not just one or two. Every person gets to feel like they belong and are a part of the system, not just one or two.

Since humanity began, two people meet, fall in love, commit to each other, bear children and create a family with the best of intentions to create a system that meets all of the needs of each family member most of the time in a balanced way. But it's simply too much to ask of any system. Errors creep in, crises arise, we try too hard in one area and not hard enough in another. Dad wants to be very involved with his children because he knows how important it is, but if the family runs into a financial crisis and he has to work two jobs to make ends meet, he sets aside some of the needs for belonging and love for more important biological needs. Or Mom's need for self-esteem is stronger than her need to correct mistakes, so she pretends that Dad isn't chronically depressed for fear of what others might think.

In the typical unhealthy family, these accumulated errors and imbalances pile up until the system attempts to create balance by forcing individual family members to take responsibility for one or two of these primary needs. This produces rigid, stereotyped roles, as described by Virginia Satir and further developed by Sharon Wegscheider-Cruse. These roles can be seductive and powerfully maintained by the dynamics in the family. As we grow up in our families, we are exposed to millions of nonverbal and verbal messages every day, creating a hypnotic process of unconscious learning. Families aren't malicious, they are simply systems.

COGNITIVE DISTORTIONS IN DYSFUNCTIONAL FAMILY ROLES

The well-known roles of Hero, Lost Child, Scapegoat/Rebel, Enabler, Victim, Princess and Little Parent, to name just a few, are simply system adaptations—attempts by the system to keep itself in some sort of balance. The problem for the individual family members is that each one of them gets short-changed by this adaptive arrangement. For example, the Family Hero gets to achieve and be valued but usually lacks the freedom to make mistakes, and certainly experiences damage in his sense of belongingness. The system has unconsciously selected him to be the bearer of the family's esteem, and so while he may appear to have scores of friends and admirers while growing up, he may secretly feel lonely and empty. He wants to be like the other children who play, have fun and feel included, but he feels different somehow. He may even feel as if he has a special mission in life, and he may quickly become seduced by all of the attention he gets for his achievements, which precludes him from feeling loved just for who he is.

When he becomes an adult, the Hero re-enacts his role by creating what appears to be a perfect marriage, the perfect job and the perfect children, but he is secretly unable to connect with others and he is driven by a terror that if he ever makes a mistake—if he is ever human—he will be rejected. Deep inside his soul he feels lonely, empty, ashamed and frightened. As he works deeply into the core of his problems and tries to step out of this painful role, the Hero will eventually encounter various cognitive distortions that help keep him stuck in the past.

In other words, with each painful childhood role that we play, there are various cognitive distortions that go along with it, and it is these cognitive distortions that we must confront if we are ever to move into adulthood. Growing up isn't just about feelings. It is also about how we think and what we do. In the words of William Shakespeare, "Thoughts are but dreams till their effects be tried." (*The Rape of Lucrece,* 1594.)

The Hero

The person who is caught in this role may carry one or more beliefs that make change difficult. She may believe that if she makes a mistake she will be discovered to be imperfect, a fraud who has been fooling everyone for years. She may believe that if she doesn't win one more award or earn one more graduate degree she will be abandoned by all those around her. Or she may believe that if she exposes her humanity her parents or children will not just be disappointed, but ruined. There is tremendous shame and fear of abandonment at the core of every dysfunctional role, but certainly these are key features of the Hero role.

The Hero must replace these beliefs with their healthier counterparts, including the belief that she can be competent and also flawed, that people can love and respect her for both her strengths and her weaknesses, and that if she shares her true self with others she will not be abandoned.

The Lost Child

A man who is still acting out this role will often believe that if he is noticed by anyone he will be ridiculed, or worse. He defended himself from a painful system in childhood by becoming invisible, and the system reinforced it because a child who is invisible doesn't require much. As the system becomes overloaded with stress, it welcomes a member who denies his needs. As an adult he may also believe that it is wrong—rude, pushy, brazen or even selfish—to have needs and make them known. It is safe to be invisible, but it is lonely and painful, too. And so he struggles in misery believing that he is unworthy of having what he wants or needs and fearing retribution if he asks.

As this person grows into adulthood, he can choose new beliefs, such as the belief that to want something is a sign of one's uniqueness, identity and spirituality; or the belief that if he gets noticed and lets his needs be known life will respond positively some of the time; or that healthy people will not go away simply because he stands up for his rights. He can still enjoy being alone but believes that it is his responsibility to reach out and connect with others if he is to overcome chronic isolation and loneliness.

The Scapegoat/Rebel

When individual family members are unwilling to take responsibility for their own flaws, the system has no way to correct mistakes. Error in the system builds up like pressure in a steam heating system with a malfunctioning pressure-release valve, and eventually the boiler explodes. The Scapegoat/Rebel is like the pressure-release valve that blows so that the rest of the family can *appear* normal. The child who acts out in school, gets addicted to drugs or gets labeled as the "black sheep" is the one who lets the pressure out of the system and thus provides a very useful service to the family in a very damaging way. The child does not choose this role. He takes it on unconsciously, because the system needs it. And so he gets into trouble and gets blamed for all of the family's woes when, in fact, it is the family's pain that is causing him to act out.

Angry, ashamed, defiant and troubled, this child knows at some level that the system is in pain but lacks the adult resources to change it. As an adult, a Scapegoat/Rebel believes that if he stops being angry and defiant he will be hurt irreparably. Or he believes that no one will believe that the rest of the system is damaged. Frustrated, agitated and alone, he also believes that if he admits his own flaws the system will gang up on him and blame him for everything, which it does anyway. Worse, he believes unconsciously that if there isn't someone to blame, the system itself will "blow up," leaving him and everyone else abandoned.

Eventually he begins to believe that he is indeed bad to the core, different, the "bad seed." In working with his belief system, it is important to challenge this thinking firmly and gently so that he can replace those old beliefs with the truth—that he is not bad to the core, that there are other human beings who can see the dysfunction in the rest of the family, and that he no longer has to let the pressure off of the system because it is each family member's job to do that for themselves. And in the end, he must take adult responsibility for the harm that he causes to self and others.

The Enabler

This is the person who as a child tried to keep the family together by taking responsibility for her parents or siblings in ways that are inappropriate for a child to be allowed to do. The system relied on her to do whatever it took to keep the family intact, including protecting or covering up addictive and abusive behavior. A child will be drawn to this role because without her parents she would literally die; it is a matter of simple survival. But as an adult, trying to keep a system together regardless of the cost can result in untold damage. A woman covers for her husband's alcoholism for fear of losing him to divorce and instead loses him to a drunk driving accident. A man does not challenge his wife's raging, and eventually his son attempts suicide as a way out of a crazy system.

The Enabler believes that if he stops covering up and protecting abuse or addiction the system will disintegrate. He believes that if the person he loves is not protected she will disintegrate in a pool of embarrassment. He believes that he will no longer be loved or have a family if reality is embraced rather than fantasy. And thus the beliefs that must be learned are that love includes personal accountability, that some systems are better off changing even if it means divorce; and that to be loved, one does not have to sacrifice his sanity, his integrity or his own self.

The Mascot/Clown

The Mascot/Clown is enlisted to distract the system from its pain by being entertaining but basically powerless. The system sees him as funny and delightful but not to be taken seriously. The more charming and funny he can be the less the family has to take itself seriously. It is an embarrassing role to play, because it is a very seductive one in which the child is unconsciously used by the system. A child in this role will be noticed when he is funny but will quickly learn that his deep pain and sadness inside is not worth sharing because the system can't handle any more pain. As an adult, this person must begin to believe that all of his feelings have value, that when he laughs off his own pain everyone else does, too; and that if he is ever to be taken seriously he must take himself seriously first. Deeper still, he must begin believing that there are people in the world who will acknowledge him when he isn't being funny or charming, that expressing sadness and hurt now and then is as healthy as a good sense of humor, and that power comes not just from being entertaining but also from being competent and having integrity.

The Saint

Every system needs spirituality in the broad sense of being able to admit something more powerful beyond itself. Without this ability, a system gradually degenerates into a cesspool of arrogance, grandiosity, self-importance, rigidity, intolerance and destructiveness. A malfunctioning family system will often select one of the children to act out the spirituality for it in the form of a religious piety impossible for a child to comprehend or embrace. Because sexuality and spirituality are so closely intertwined, an adult caught in this role often has deep unresolved sexual issues that may take the form of sexual blunting and denial, sexual compulsivity or sexual perpetration on others. At the very least, the Saint is one who is so disconnected from others, because of neglect or abuse, that the only relationship that feels safe is the one he has with God.

Unfortunately, spirituality isn't just about going to the mountaintop and praying alone. The other half of spirituality involves the day-to-day struggles, joys and heartaches of being in relationship with other human beings; thus The Saint's distorted belief system actually keeps him from the very spirituality that he seeks. In becoming an adult, the Saint must learn to believe that there are human beings who can be trusted enough to be in relationship with him, that there are no perfect human beings, that praying alone is only half of the solution to loneliness, that there are humans who can truly understand his loneliness and pain, and that everyone in the family is responsible for his own spirituality, not just the Saint. Lastly, he must come to grips with the painful reality that each one of us has the capacity for holiness. As he embraces these new beliefs, the

Saint not only deepens his relationships with those around him, but also with the God in whom he believes.

Mom's Little Man/Dad's Little Princess

Perhaps the most notorious, damaging and difficult role that children get caught in is the one in which the child becomes the pal or confidant to the parent. It is insidious, because it feels so good to an emotionally starved child to be that needed by a parent; and it is damaging because, until it is detected and healed, it almost universally precludes an adult's ability to have a healthy love relationship with another adult. Because it is so harmful, many professionals refer to it as the emotional or covert incest role. As powerful as a child may feel as he sits and listens to his parent's secret longings, pains and troubles, being seduced into this position by a parent can only cause grief and terrible distress later on, because it lays down a pattern of seduction and objectification that is very hard to identify.

An adult who is Mom's Little Man or Dad's Little Princess believes that he is more special than others, that he has more power than he really has, that romantic love is about caring for wounded people who look less powerful than him but who are actually much more powerful, that it is his job to heal others rather than theirs, and that there is no way to get close to a lover other than through neurotic bonds. In healing these patterns, one must come to believe that it is possible to love another who is an equal rather than more powerful, that it is not our job to rescue every wounded soul on the planet, that we can be in relationship with someone who is healthy, and that we should stay away from people who harm us rather than being drawn to them like a moth to a flame.

THINKING BEYOND PAINFUL ROLES

Some therapists believe that the only way to heal childhood wounds is to repeatedly do what is called "feelings work" in which we replay our childhood pain, symbolically tell our perpetrators how we have been hurt and how we won't allow it in the future, and grieve our losses. But sooner or later we must think our way into adulthood, too. Thomas Huxley said that "What we call rational grounds for our beliefs are often extremely irrational attempts to justify our instincts." (*On the Natural Inequality of Man, 1890.*) We must look at our distorted belief systems clearly and make a conscious decision to believe differently, and then we must begin to act on those new beliefs. Only then can we release the past and fully embrace the soul of adulthood.

Chapter 14

VICTIM TO ADULT

Put your trust in God, but mind to keep your powder dry.

Oliver Cromwell
At the Battle of Edgehill, 1642

Back in the early 1970s, a good friend of ours took a job as director of a small program for developmentally disabled children in a rural community near her husband's military base. She took on various professional jobs as he was transferred from place to place around the United States. This job afforded her the opportunity to share her tremendous energy, creativity and enthusiasm with the local community while she got challenging teaching experiences that rivaled anything she could have had in a college-level practicum. It was a mutually satisfying arrangement between her and this small group of parents who deeply appreciated her very successful efforts to help their children.

Despite the often slow and painful progress exhibited by these children, she tackled each new day with boundless energy and optimism as she worked with parents, brainstormed with her inexperienced staff, and read journal articles and books that might give her new techniques or insights that could help the children move forward developmentally. She was the kind of program director about whom every parent dreams, and the parents grew to appreciate and love her for all that she did. They worked hard for her, too, because while she was filled with hope and positive energy throughout her own day, she also expected the parents of her children to have hope and to work hard as well. She was a very good role model for them.

And then one day someone from her board of directors accused her of stealing petty cash from her own office. This was laughable to everyone who knew her given her financial stability and her compulsive honesty. Of course, it wasn't really about petty cash at all—it was about a petty board of directors who believed that this young woman was becoming too powerful—and thus it was really about fear. Realizing that there was little she could do in the face of such powerful small-town politics, she reluctantly resigned and for several months thereafter was in a deep grieving process. She heard rumors that the parents were very upset by the board's actions, but she chose to accept the reality of politics and to try to heal as best she could so that she could regain her emotional balance and put her energies into a more productive undertaking.

She didn't have to wait long. After a few months without her, a group of parents from her former program and some from the neighboring community got together and asked her to start up a new center. Although her wounds had begun to heal and the prospect of starting all over again initially seemed overwhelming, their encouragement and appreciation were so clear and powerful that she rose to the challenge and began anew. By the time her husband was transferred 3,000 miles away to another base, she had not only created another wonderfully successful program but had trained a new director and staff who were able to carry on her work after she left.

We recently spoke to this woman about this experience that happened over a quarter of a century ago, and to this day, she has very little energy tied up in how she "got even" or "got revenge" with people who had made her life so painful for a moment in her history. She still speaks with some animation about the experience, but her animation is tied up more with how she managed to rebound, the choices that she made to release the struggle and then to re-engage her life in a new way, and the energy that she put into the new school. Her memories are mostly fond ones even though it was such a painful time for her when it was happening. She chooses to focus on the children and parents she helped and on how much she learned rather than on how awful it was when she was unfairly accused.

BEYOND VICTIMISM

Life isn't fair all the time, but it is filled with inspiring stories like this. There are many people who have the inner resources to interpret adversity in a way that permits them to move through it rather than to become a victim of it. Where we choose to put our energy is extremely important, because it will determine whether or not we remain bogged down in regret, bitterness and dissatisfaction when life doesn't seem fair to us. The tragedy of victimism is that the person caught in it wants to be like the woman above but doesn't believe he or she can do it, or worse, explains away that woman's success by saying that she simply "got lucky." But we all know what Gary Player said: "The harder you work, the luckier you get."

Moving beyond victimism can be one of the more painful, frightening and rewarding things any human being can do. It is painful and frightening, because anyone caught in it has, by definition, been in it a long time for some very legitimate reasons. A man stays in a critical, shaming relationship with his partner not because he wants to be dominated but because he fears abandonment and fears for his children's emotional well-being. He stays because of his shame, which tells him he isn't worthy of a better relationship. And he stays because of confused beliefs he learned a long time ago—that one must always be nice, always put others' feelings first, never stand out, never stand up and never stand in the way of anyone else. These longstanding patterns are not just swept away with the brush of a hand. They have teeth and they don't want to let go of us, which means that we must actively engage them and replace them with healthier habits.

BEYOND VICTIMISM AT WORK AND PLAY

Habits of adulthood are very different from habits of victimism. Because a grown-up adult has moved beyond extremes in thinking, feeling and behavior, her power is effective and balanced rather than unfocused and out of control, which means that her actions make things happen in socially appropriate ways. Rather than waiting for people to read her mind and benevolently give her what she wants, or getting it no matter who she hurts, she will clarify what she really wants and then find accountable ways to go after her goals. Dissatisfied with her job and seeing no way to improve it from inside her corporate department, she may gradually develop and then present a comprehensive plan for a new product line or service. She will know how to sell it and how to gain political support for it along the way, or will ask people who do know how. Convinced that she has a successful idea that fires her own imagination, she knows that even if it isn't accepted within the company, all of her work will not be in vain. Once the plan is fully developed and refined, she can either take it to another company or start a business on her own. And most of all, she understands that just because she is convinced it is a great idea does not mean that anyone else will be.

An adult also has optimism tempered with realism. If he wants a first-class vacation to Europe but doesn't have the money, he either waits until he has it or accepts the disappointment and goes tourist. If he were caught in victimism, his disappointment would overwhelm him and he would be angry, bitter and blame someone else for his inability to go first-class. Adults have a unique balance of activism, patience, wisdom and acceptance of the way life is. Being an adult does not mean getting everything we want, but because we select our battles carefully and engage them wisely, we optimize our chances of winning many of them. When we don't succeed, we are able to accept our disappointment with gracious regret and then move forward again.

BEYOND VICTIMISM IN RELATIONSHIPS

Grown-ups also understand that it takes two to tango, so that no matter how much they might feel that it is totally someone else's fault, they know this can't be true. Being effective and competent, they focus much more on asking what part they are playing in a problem rather than constantly looking to blame the other person. When blame is placed totally outside of us, it bonds us to victimism. There are no other options, because the very nature of blame forces our energy outside of ourselves, away from the source of power and change that resides deep within us.

It is a wonder to behold when two people finally take responsibility for their own part in a relationship breakdown, instead of blaming each other. A man says, "When we fight, I tend to criticize her, which really makes it worse. She gets understandably defensive and then it just escalates." When he owns his part, it frees her up to say, "When we fight, I get really defensive because of my shame. I need to admit when I'm wrong." When she admits it, he feels less like criticizing her, and the two of them mutually reverse the downward spiral of bickering, turning it into an upward progression of intimacy.

MOVING OUT OF THE VICTIM ROLE

Edward Everett Hale said, "I am only one, but still I am one. I cannot do everything, but still I can do something; and because I cannot do everything I will not refuse to do the something that I can do." When we are caught in our victimism, it is like pulling teeth to take personal responsibility for our lives, but it can be done. A man came into therapy with a long list of complaints about his current and former employers. He had an even longer list of what he described as despicable, incompetent therapists with whom he had worked. Over a seven-year period he had seen ten different therapists and each attempt at working through his issues ended on the same sour note—the therapist was inept, unethical, incompetent, abusive, controlling, uncaring and poorly trained. Granted, there are incompetent therapists, but the chances of getting ten bad ones out of ten are as likely as winning the lottery, and the chances of learning "nothing" from them are even slimmer. And so we carefully began by setting some very clear therapeutic guidelines with this man as we steeled ourselves for the predictable anger that was soon to follow.

Perhaps because he was tired of his victimism and perhaps because we stumbled on a therapeutic approach that seemed to engage him, he was able to stick with therapy long enough to begin taking some responsibility for his disappointments. What he discovered was that no matter where he was employed or with whom he worked in therapy it would never be perfect. The ability to discern this truth is one of the key differences between an adult and a wounded child.

Rather than getting into power struggles with him over who was victimizing him or not, we worked with his victim belief system by gently asking him if he could identify any small instances in his life where people had treated him well. At first his victim filter made this task difficult, but as we worked with him, he was able to discover more and more examples of positive interactions throughout his life. And each time he presented extreme statements such as "All people are out to hurt me," or "my life never works out," we helped him move away from the extremes by looking at the examples he had listed. Eventually, he began to replace generalizations and beliefs about life expressed by "always," "never," "all people," and "no one," with words like "some," and "sometimes." From there he was able to dismantle the victim filter that had protected him, so that he could see with the mature eyes of an adult.

An adult has choices and knows it, whereas a victim has choices but doesn't believe it. As Diane Naas says, "Just because someone asks you a question doesn't mean you have to answer it." When we know we have choices, we can make even a poor situation better while keeping some semblance of dignity and personal power. Caught in a difficult job due to a soft employment market, an adult can find scores of ways to make the job more tolerable, knowing that someday she will be able to move on. Embracing our capacity to choose is essential in leaving our victimism behind. But finding those choices often means that we must accept tradeoffs, which is another key part of adulthood. A victim will look for all-or-nothing solutions to problems—his partner must change all 15 things on his list of requested changes or he won't stay in the relationship. This rigidity guarantees that he will never have a good relationship with anyone, because no one will be able to meet all of his demands.

Victimism feeds itself, and adulthood feeds itself, too. If you look at any tight-knit social group from this vantage point, you may notice that people who blame everyone else spend a lot of time with people who also blame everyone else. Those who feel powerless gather in the same area at a party. Those who believe that life is done to them find each other. On the other hand, people who take responsibility for their lives tend to gather at parties. Those who believe they have choices and are willing to take risks are drawn to one another. It is therefore essential for us to learn from those who are healthier than us if we are ever to move from the bondage of victimism to the peace and power of adulthood.

If you consider the extremes that we discussed in Chapter Two, then you will understand another reason why it is so hard to move from victim to adult. Whenever a person moves from the extremes toward balance, it initially feels like he is swinging way out to the other extreme. Of course, some people do swing to the other extreme for awhile, but that's another matter. A man who doesn't say "no" for fear of alienating others will feel cruel and cold-hearted when he first says "no" to someone's request. But as he experiments with setting these limits, and as he tests out their appropriateness by talking with others, he eventually finds that middle ground. It also helps when he begins identifying with healthier people instead of criticizing them as he did when immersed in his victimism.

THE WORLD OF ADULTHOOD

Becoming an adult, therefore, requires that we identify with the world of adulthood, and leave behind our earlier identification with the victim role, which is scary. The world of adulthood is more complex, more hopeful, more soulful and deeper. A victim pretends that she can create a simplistic world without politics and is forever angry and frustrated because there can't be such a thing. She is angry at her friends, angry at her therapist, angry at the government, angry at her church and angry at her neighbors, because none of them is doing exactly as she wishes. Politics arise as soon as there are two people under one roof for more than 30 minutes; an adult accepts this fact and learns to live in the political world with as much integrity and respect as she can muster.

An adult knows that all relationships end, and the sadness of that truth opens life up to all of its infinite joys. The victim who fights with those endings destroys, ignores or denies the peace that comes with the accepted sorrows. An adult can be deeply intimate with another person when she has met her own depth. This includes self-knowledge, acceptance of self-limits, a strong internal structure, appropriate anger to set boundaries and create identity, and the willingness to risk being hurt coupled with the wisdom to not get hurt too much. A victim fights to be deeply intimate, but lacking a clear self, ends up getting lost, getting hurt or hurting others in the process.

Childhood can be a time of innocence, magic, wonder and safety or it can be a time of pain and loneliness. Regardless of what it was, there is a time to be a child and there is a time to grow up. When we decide that it is time to put aside the pain and heartache of our victimism, then we have also decided to finish our business with our childhoods and move on. It is a sad time, but also a time of renewed promise and fulfillment as we embrace this part of the soul of adulthood.

Chapter 15

LOVE, POWER AND GRACIOUSNESS

It is not ill-bred to adopt a high manner with the great and powerful, but it is vulgar to lord it over humble people.

Aristotle
The Nicomachean Ethics, c. 340 B.C.

Confucius said "Only the truly kind person knows how to love and how to hate," which for some of us is as perplexing today as it was in 500 B.C. Maintaining the fragile balance between love and hate, grace and power, and revenge and forgiveness is a fundamental aspect of the intimate side of the adult soul. For many years we have counseled people that love and hate are part of the same complex bond that connects us to each other, and that without our healthy anger it is very difficult to experience deeper intimacy with another. The closer we get to each other it is more likely we will step on each other's toes, and it is more likely we will lose our identities in the attempt to fuse with our beloved unless we have access to our anger. Anger is there to protect us, to set boundaries, to provide resistance, and as such, it is essential for deep love.

In another book, we defined intimacy as the ability to maintain a relationship with another person without losing our identity in the process. We have often said that deep love occurs when we connect with each other at the level of our weakness, but this is only true as long as we do not expect our loved one to repair that weakness. A man confides in his partner that he feels frightened of an upcoming meeting with an associate, and he thus exposes his vulnerability to her. He is a powerful person at work yet he is a human being like her, with fears and vulnerabilities. He has let down all of his normal self-protections and has opened himself up to shame, criticism and rejection. She acknowledges that he is scared, that he feels "little;" but she does not try to remove it, belittle it, compare it or imply that he is weak and she is strong, because she respects his vulnerability and trusts that he simply needs her to hear him. They both maintain their power and dignity in this tiny moment of deep intimacy, and they set the stage for her to share a moment of weakness with him in the future. He takes care of his fear in his own way, as an adult, but with the added confidence of knowing that she does not view his vulnerability as a defect.

Love is an ongoing dance, struggle and balancing act between self and other, between lover and beloved. Too little resistance and the relationship flows into smothering and fusion, too much resistance and it ricochets out into isolation and emotional poverty. Too much care results in helplessness and resentment, not enough care results in emptiness and shame. In the end, two people who "do everything right" but who are unable to share at the level of their weakness live in a practical but lifeless void.

GRACIOUSNESS

There are many meanings for the word "gracious," but here we wish to focus on two from the Oxford English

Dictionary (1971). The first is: "Disposed to show or dispense grace, merciful, compassionate," and the second is: "Characterized by or exhibiting kindness or courtesy; kindly, benevolent, courteous." Some would say that we have lost the capacity for graciousness in our society and that we are so literal and practical we have driven the magic and tenderness right out of our lives. But then we encounter a person who is deeply gracious, and we are startled by our appreciation of him, which shows that we long for graciousness in our lives even as we fumble for the words and images to describe it. We do not take graciousness lightly. We just aren't sure what it is or how to do it, because we lacked models of graciousness when we were young.

A woman prepares her home for holiday visitors and reflects with care on the personalities and idiosyncrasies of each guest without judging them. One likes fine wine, another exercises regularly, another requires extra privacy and another likes to meet new people and engage in spirited conversation. She would never assume that everyone was just like herself. She puts her special touches all around her home, because it is an expression of her inner self and is thus a subtle way of reaching into another's consciousness without intruding. When her guests arrive, she makes them feel at home by her kindness and detachment. She doesn't hover because it makes people uncomfortable, but she remains unconsciously attuned to the needs of her guests without sacrificing her own needs.

She includes her guests in her own holiday plans and celebrations whenever it is fitting to do so, but does not push her plans on others, always leaving each guest plenty of room to say, "I'd love to join you and your friends for dinner but I think I'd better take some time for myself this evening." She is kind and courteous. When someone oversteps his bounds, she is able to respond without hurting his dignity. A guest who tries to stay too long would not be confronted and told that he is being rude. She might simply use her own vulnerability to avoid exposing the obvious vulnerability of her inappropriate guest by saying, "I'm having a wonderful time talking with you, but I think I'm losing some of my youthful stamina. Would you mind terribly if I retired for the evening, and we could continue our conversation at a later date?" Perhaps John Milton described this woman best with these words from *Paradise Lost:* "Grace was in all her steps, Heaven in her eye, In every gesture dignity and love."

Of course, graciousness can be an insincere, affected performance intended to make oneself appear superior rather than as a genuine expression of respect for the dignity of other souls, but then it would not be the kind of graciousness that we have defined here. Anyone can read an etiquette book, but it is the struggle to acquire empathy, respect, maturity and depth of soul that allows us to be truly gracious. Following the rules of etiquette without developing one's inner graciousness would be a hollow gesture at best.

Graciousness is essential in love relationships. A man and woman are having a disagreement about something and as it becomes more heated the man suddenly becomes aware that the woman is tired and that her emotional reserves are low. He detects a point of weakness in her which could give him an edge in the argument, but instead of trying to win he abruptly changes course and says to her, "You know, I think you're right about this. I wasn't looking at it from the same angle that you were. It makes sense to me now." His graciousness releases the tension between them and allows her to feel heard and understood, which is exactly what someone needs when they are tired and their emotional reserves are low. He could have won but decided to exercise tact, compassion and mercy, which is what being gracious is all about. The great issues of the day can be debated later. Hurting a person's spirit is not worth needing to be right all the time.

It is said that we always hurt the ones we love, a statement we see confirmed with unnecessary frequency in our culture. But as people mature and deepen in spirit, they are able to take to heart and put into practice these wise and gracious words of Oliver Wendell Holmes:

> *Do not flatter yourself that friendship authorizes you to say disagreeable things to your intimates. The nearer you come into relation with a person, the more necessary tact and courtesy become. Except in cases which are rare, leave your friend to learn unpleasant things from his enemies; they are ready enough to tell him.*

GRACIOUSNESS AND POWER

Graciousness and power are inextricably intertwined. The power to which we refer is not necessarily measured by wealth, status or political influence, although these may be a part of one's overall power. This kind of power is measured by the clarity of one's spirit, the depth of one's soul, the strength of one's character and the quality of one's mercy. A truly gracious person is powerful, while an artificially gracious person is not, even though they may appear to be. A powerful person does not use her power to harm others or to gain unfair advantage over them, whereas a weak person is always looking for a way to diminish others in some fashion. Mature power is about protection, integrity, honor, respect, care, wisdom, tenderness and compassion. Immature power is about fear, greed, revenge, narcissism, harm, selfishness, want and bitterness. One of the most dynamic and energizing aspects of adulthood is our struggle to balance power and graciousness, to temper one with the other.

Graciousness Without Power

When a person tries to be gracious without first having tapped into the protective power of her soul, she may find herself feeling angry and bitter much of the time. Anger empowers and protects so that the kind person is not taken for granted. Without healthy anger, our attempts at graciousness will fall short, coming to rest at the more immature level of "indiscriminate niceness." This distortion of kindness directly contradicts the wisdom of Confucius cited above. Graciousness does not flow from our fear of rejection; it flows despite that fear. True kindness is not a cleverly disguised attempt to prevent others from hurting us, nor is it an attempt to buy affection or admiration. It is simply an attempt to affirm the spirit of another human being for no reason other than because we care about each other's dignity. Erik Erikson said:

> We must stand ready to expect and to respond to human love in any of our fellow men so long as they do not set out

to kill that human dignity in us without which we could not really love anybody. For only people with equal dignity can love each other.

Graciousness without power is just another way to describe victimhood or martyrdom. An adult does not feel comfortable around someone who has sacrificed his identity for the sake of a relationship and who therefore fawns, hovers or grovels in the name of "niceness." The recipient of such behavior is placed in the unwanted and painful position of having to bear witness to and participate in another's unacknowledged embarrassment. It is also a double bind in which we find ourselves angry at someone who appears to be nice on the outside, until we unwind the bind by recognizing that the other person is actually manipulating us, as in the following interchange:

"Can I wash your car for you?"

"No, actually, I was looking forward to doing it myself. It's one of those personal things I like to do on my own."

"Really, it's no trouble at all. I enjoy washing cars. Why don't you just rest up for the party this evening."

"Well, I was rather looking forward to washing my car."

"But I'd really like to do it for you."

"That's very kind of you, but I choose to do it myself."

Power Without Graciousness

The Maori people of New Zealand have a saying that goes something like this: "Never judge a man by how he behaves outside of his own hut," which is another way of saying that we tend to hurt the ones we love. Graciousness is not confined to how we treat people in public. When it is, then we are really talking about an artificial performance rather than a characteristic of soulfulness deep within ourselves. A truly gracious person will respond to the human dignity inside of each person he encounters, whether at home or in public. If he detects weakness, ineptness or vulnerability within you, he will respond in a way that honors who you are, not who he would like you to become, as long as you do not "set out to kill that human dignity" in him that is required for love.

During a therapy session a man told us of a transforming experience he had while at a cocktail party connected with his job. He was very uncomfortable in social settings and this was an especially painful one for him, because most of the people there were more powerful and better educated than him. He felt very much out of place as he wandered from group to group trying to find a way into one of the conversations but never succeeding. As he stood at the bar and ordered another ice water, when out of nowhere a well-dressed gentleman appeared beside him and said, "I'm always uncomfortable at these blasted things. I'd much rather be at home watching a movie with my wife." Our client immediately felt at ease and struck up a pleasant conversation with this man that lasted until the man had to go up to the podium to receive an award. It turned out that this gracious gentleman was the most powerful person in the room, and our client's brief encounter with the man transformed his beliefs about people who possess wealth and power. With an innocent and grateful smile our client said, "I once believed that all powerful people were arrogant, aloof and hurtful, but this man showed me otherwise."

Power without graciousness is patronizing and condescending, and is, therefore, just another way to describe an offender, perpetrator or manipulator. With every ounce of newly-acquired power comes greater responsibility to treat the less powerful with respect, compassion and care. An ungraciously powerful person will play on the power differential between the two of you. He will be an emotional or physical predator preying on your weaknesses and belittling your strengths until you are drowning in a pool of shame. He will always be right even when he isn't, by simply intimidating you. He may cleverly treat people outside of his own hut with artificial respect, but in his very intimate relationships he will be overbearing, controlling or worse. If you are in love with this person, you will quickly find that he never shows his own weakness and that it is never safe for you to show yours. To use our words from earlier in this chapter, the two of you will be unable to connect at the level of your weakness, and so you will be unable to enjoy the experience of deep love for one another.

LOVE, POWER AND GRACIOUSNESS

Graciousness requires time, effort and thoughtfulness, which are at a premium in our fast-paced society. When we are always in a hurry, we don't have the time to stop and notice how the other person is reacting or what they might want or need, and we certainly won't notice what we feel, want or need, either. The result is that we feel shortchanged and empty in our relationships, which eventually turn into feelings of powerlessness, bitterness and vengefulness.

Compassion, mercy, kindness and love must be nurtured like rare orchids in a nursery. Powerful lovers

cherish their dependency upon one another while protecting their independence at the same time. They fight
fairly and openly, stopping short of capitalizing on each
other's vulnerability. They treat each other with kindness
and respect, and they harbor a deep abiding appreciation
for the mystery of the love that they share. As Samuel
Johnson wrote in 1773: "Gratitude is a fruit of great culti-
vation; you do not find it among gross people."

Each of us struggles with the relationship between
power, love and graciousness, whether it be in a marriage,
a business partnership, a friendship or a more distant association. Sometimes, especially if our dignity is at stake, we
must take Confucius' words to heart and be angry, dispens-
ing with the tact and courtesy suggested by Holmes.
Sometimes we need to release the outrage in our hearts for
the sake of our own or others' security. Love is complex and
human relationships are sometimes unfathomable. The soul
is not black and white, it is not linear and it is not static. But
without an ideal for which to strive we are like ships adrift
in a sea of emotion and primitive, reactive, defensive urges.
Regardless of how confusing our relationships may get, and
no matter how hard it is to know the best way to treat one
another at times, we still find ourselves gently charting a
course back toward the timeless description of love written
by Paul in his letter to the Corinthians. In these words we
find welcome direction and comfort as well as the beginnings of peace deep within our souls:

> Love suffers long and is kind; love does not envy; love does
> not parade itself, is not puffed up; does not behave rudely,
> does not seek its own, is not provoked, thinks no evil; does
> not rejoice in iniquity, but rejoices in the truth; bears all

things, believes all things, hopes all things, endures all things. Love never fails.

Chapter 16

RELEASING

To everything there is a season, and a time to every purpose under heaven.

Ecclesiastes 3:1

"There is a time to be born and a time to die; a time to plant and a time to harvest; a time to kill and a time to heal; a time to break down, and a time to build up; a time to weep, and a time to laugh; a time to mourn, and a time to dance; a time to cast away stones, and a time to gather stones together; a time to embrace, and a time to refrain from embracing; a time to get, and a time to lose; a time to keep, and a time to cast away; a time to rend, and a time to sew; a time to keep silence, and a time to speak; a time to love, and a time to hate; a time of war, and a time of peace."

To everything there is a season, and a time to every purpose under heaven. A time to try and a time to quit. A time to begin and a time to end. A time to struggle and a time to release the struggle, and then move on. Along the often foggy border between struggling and releasing rests wisdom—the elusive quality that separates the impetuousness of youth from the gracious power of adulthood. As we acknowledged in a previous chapter, to struggle is to affirm our existence, so that without struggle we would literally no longer be alive. But to live more fully, we must also be capable of releasing parts of our struggle so that we can open our lives to greater depth and meaning. The balance between resistance and release becomes ever more exquisite as we mature.

There is great wisdom in the saying, "He won the battle but lost the war." If we analyze this wisdom literally, it refers to the fact that in war a commander might decide to send all of his troops and supplies into one battle in the belief that if he wins this one he will crush his enemy and be done with it. But he miscalculates how much it will take to win this battle, and he underestimates his enemy's overall strength and troop size. He wins the battle only to discover that his enemy has begun another attack on a distant front, but our commander no longer has the troops or supplies to defend himself. Depleted of energy, manpower and supplies, the commander is soon surrounded and ultimately defeated. Although he won the previous battle, he has lost the war because of his strategic miscalculation.

Sometimes we simply do not have enough information, resources or power to win our personal wars. But sometimes we lose because we lack the strategic wisdom to know when to struggle and when to let go of the struggle. And some of us engage in so many battles that our resources are continually on the verge of collapse. There are times when we must reach down into the depths of our souls and ask, "Is it worth it?" As we mature and accumulate wisdom the fog enshrouding the border between struggle and release slowly lifts, and we are better able to discern that giving up a struggle does not necessarily mean giving up. As we noted in our first book, some of us "try so hard that we lose, while others try so little that we never live life at all."

REACHING INTO THE TORNADO

If you have come this far in the present book, you have already read several stories of men and women who were finally able to let go of a struggle and who were subsequently rewarded with a deeper, more peaceful, more powerful life. These include the man who longed to return to the place of his youth; the woman who dreamt of the gossamer veil; and the man, the woman and the sea. What you may also have noticed as you read those stories is that in each case the person was caught in an inner turmoil from which he believed he would never be free. In each case, something changed deep inside of the person as a result of an active struggle. A decision was made to be open to the possibility of seeing life differently, of feeling things differently or of acting differently. It was this simple willingness to be open to a different outlook that signaled the beginning of the releasing process within his or her own soul.

In the beginning, many people describe this process as one of being trapped inside of a powerful, incomprehensible tornado. They describe a massive whirlwind of conflicting fears, desires, hopes, dreams, needs, wants and responsibilities—feelings, beliefs, and actions crashing into one another as they are whipped around by gale-force winds. One man was nearly suicidal inside of a maelstrom containing his desire to change careers and his fears of letting down his family and friends if he ever gave up being a physician to pursue his lifelong dream of becoming an artist. A woman was tossed about violently, like a tiny boat in a hurricane, as she struggled with the decision to have children or not.

As the struggle continues along the outer layers of each person's soul, he begins to move back from the center of the tornado to gain a new perspective. Many people describe this as a "stepping away," or a "moving away" from the inner storm, and at first it is very uncomfortable. When we have been grappling with something for a long time, our nervous systems become conditioned to the feeling of conflict and struggle. Our belief systems become convinced that if we let go of one part of ourselves to nurture another part, we will cease to exist altogether. It is natural to fear change and loss. But along with the discomfort comes an incredible sense of relief and peace. A human being can struggle for only so long before either succumbing to the intense stress or beginning to let go. The new perspective that comes with stepping away from the storm is exhilarating as we realize that there might be another way to live.

A woman described it this way. She stepped away from the middle of the turmoil swirling around inside of her and immediately felt some relief. Then she felt guilty and afraid that she was being irresponsible, that she was giving up. The tornado continued to threaten her, hovering closer and closer, trying to suck her back into its powerful winds. She chose to remain outside the tornado despite her discomfort. Then she carefully reached inside the tornado and with just the right finesse, she plucked the key piece of the conflict out of the tornado. Just as suddenly, the tornado collapsed and dissipated before her very eyes. She grieved then, knowing that it was the beginning of the end of this era of her life. She grieved the parts of her life that she was releasing into the universe. She grieved the parts of her life that would be left unfinished as she moved forward to live more fully. And yes, she grieved the loss of the confusing intensity which had been such a close and comfortable companion for so many years. As we let go of the old way to make room for a new perspective, there will inevitably be a powerful feeling of grief that washes over us for a while. She said, "I reached into the jaws of a beast and reclaimed my destiny."

ALL GOOD THINGS . . .

A man said, "If only we could go back to the first few years of our marriage. Those were the best years of our lives." A woman laments the pending completion of an audit that she is doing for one of her favorite corporations and says with fond regret, "It is so hard to say goodbye for now. I know that I'll see you again next year, but in my heart I wish I could work with all of you permanently." Then she smiles with a chuckle of selfconsciousness and says in a warm but businesslike manner, "Well then, I'll see all of you next year."

Many years ago a wise person said to us, *"And remember, all relationships end."* When we first heard this, we were confused. Could this be true? What about really good relationships? We struggled with it, intellectualizing about it, defending against the truth of it. After all, we were young, and when you are young you want to believe that nothing good must end as long as you apply your energy and talents properly. In youth, we carry the personal fable of our own immortality and omnipotence. But the person was correct, despite our youthful mental gymnastics. All relationships eventually end, a fact that stirs up the deepest fear abiding in the hearts of every human being—the fear of being alone.

It can be sad and frightening at first to embrace this truth about endings, but then it also opens the possibilities of an indescribable subtlety of appreciation and clarity of awareness about life. But this awareness that we will someday be without our best friend or our lover, either through changes in life trajectory or through death, can only bring heightened appreciation and deepened intimacy if we have passed through the doors into adulthood. As we do, we release the unbearable infantile terror of being left alone and replace it with a bearable adult fear tempered by sorrow. It is then that the strings are tuned for the delicate balance between life and death, love and loss, companionship and loneliness, which allows us to experience ecstasy.

All good things must come to an end, because life has rhythms that include beginnings and endings. The innocence and safety of childhood pass as we move into adulthood. Our children grow up and move out of the house, leaving us with an empty nest. The new car we bought loses its newness and gradually gets old. The warm nights of summer are followed by the frigid days of winter. And the magic of a Sunday afternoon spent reminiscing with close friends, huddled around a cozy fire, gives way to the realities of work on Monday. This is part of the struggle, disappointment and resistance that life offers us so that we can learn to appreciate what we have in the moment, and thereby continually deepen.

RELEASING OLD STRUGGLES

Releasing old struggles can be especially challenging. In our twenties, it is natural to seek the perfect mate who will completely understand us and meet all of our needs without effort or disappointment. This is natural because we do not let go of the myths of childhood easily. A child wants to believe that his parents are flawless despite their flaws, and so that is what he believes. In our mother's womb, everything was taken care of without struggle, and it is this myth that we hang onto for quite some time. As we move into our thirties or forties, we slowly learn that this is a myth. We discover that our parents weren't perfect, but with that discovery comes acceptance of our own shortcomings. We realize that being in the womb was perfectly safe but it had its limitations—after all, how much wisdom, consciousness, identity and deeper intimacy did we have when we were still in the womb? The risks of coming out into the world and facing reality are great, but the rewards are even greater.

A woman we knew struggled with her mother for many years. Her mother was an unhappy person who had not been able to move forward into adulthood because of the pain that she endured as a little girl. She was controlling and manipulative with her children and perceived her children to be on earth to make her feel better. Each time this woman tried to move out into the world to claim her adult life, her mother would threaten to withdraw her love from her daughter. She would pout, refuse to have contact with her daughter and criticize her for not honoring her appropriately.

They had a longstanding conflict over this woman's right to privacy, punctuated by her mother looking through her purse, snooping through her mail, telling her how she should raise her children, demanding that she spend inordinate amounts of time with her and criticizing her for how she managed her career. When she was 38 years old, this woman was ready to live her life differently. She had given her mother the keys to her house so that her mother could water her plants while she was on vacation. Unbeknownst to her, her mother made an extra set of keys. A few weeks after returning from vacation, this woman went home from work early and discovered her mother inside her house, rummaging through her personal effects.

Her mother made excuses and threatened withdrawal of the relationship if her daughter tried to object. The woman struggled valiantly with this dilemma for many months. She asked her mother to surrender the keys, but her mother never got around to doing it. She talked frankly with her mother about her rights and responsibilities in an attempt to appeal to her mother's sense of propriety, but that didn't change things either. All the while, this woman carried a deep abiding terror that if she set an effective boundary with her mother on this issue, her mother would simply reject her permanently. And then she finally surrendered and released the struggle.

After sharing her conflict and her fears with people who would understand and support her, and after weighing the costs of keeping things the same against changing this pattern, she finally had the locks to her house changed. She never told her mother about it; she simply changed the locks and waited for the fallout. But it never materialized. Somehow her mother sensed that the battle was over, that her daughter had become an adult, and that her manipulative power would no longer be effective. There was an uneasiness between them for a few weeks after she changed the locks, but from then on her mother treated her differently. She had faced the absolute terror of losing the person who had given birth to her and who had kept her alive when she was an infant, and she decided that adulthood with sadness was far better than being stuck in infancy filled with shame and rage. By taking the risk to release the struggle and move on, this woman was able to maintain her relationship with her mother while passing through the door to her own adult world.

LISTENING TO THE SEASONS

In our work, we find many people who live with the nearly constant dread that the good things happening in their lives will not continue and that the bad things will never end. Living this way is quite painful, and rather common, especially for those of us who had troubled childhoods. Without being cleansed and healed deep inside of us, it is as if all of the pain and disappointment from those childhood wounds accumulate over time, so that we are left with a belief that nothing will ever work out the way that we want. When something does work out for us, we tend to confuse the normal rhythms of life with some faceless being's brutal or punitive wish to deprive us of the long sought happiness for which we have struggled so gallantly. Indeed, it is a difficult way to live. But it doesn't have to be this way, if only we can begin to think a little differently about the matter, if only we can move away from the extremes.

To everything there is a season. There is a time to try to convince a loved one that she needs help with her alcoholism, and there is a time to let go of it and move on with our own lives. There is a time to try to make our parents understand how they may have hurt us when we were children, and there is a time to let go of it and simply accept them for who they are. There is a time to file a lawsuit when we feel we have been wronged, and there is a time to accept the fact that even if our feelings are in line with reality, we might still be better off moving ahead in life. When we release a longstanding struggle we lose a hope or a dream that may have been very dear to us, but we also release waves of new energy and possibilities we never imagined before. When we pass through the doors to adulthood, we are allowed to experience that fragile, exquisite tension between control and surrender that makes life so magnificent and mysterious.

Chapter 17

APPRECIATION

Our present joys are sweeter for past pain.

George Granville
The British Enchanters, 1706

The more deeply spiritual we become, and the more deeply connected we become with our innermost souls, the more we are able to appreciate the ordinary aspects of life. One of the true joys of being an adult is the ability to appreciate the simple fact of being alive. It is not trite. People who have this ability have earned it, for it does not come easily. A woman who experienced tremendous tragedy in her life came to make sense of its nuances and meanings and messages, and ultimately said, "I have seen so much sorrow in my life, but I have endured; and now it is a smile, a tear, a bird singing and the very light of day that warms my heart. My life is blessed beyond measure."

It is easy to talk about the importance of appreciation, but it is another thing to embrace it and work it into one's soul. Many of us still seem to cling to the notion that we can have it all, and if we don't, we complain about our unhappiness. Many of us take each other for granted as we strive to acquire more and more of something, anything, that we believe will make us just a little bit happier. A bigger house, perhaps? A new spouse? Different friends? An exciting new vacation spot that nobody else has heard of yet? We are on never-ending spiritual quests as if our established institutions had suddenly been mysteriously drained of their wisdom.

It is troubling to witness this floundering and flailing in which so many of us are engaged. It is as if we try to continuously re-create our collective beliefs so that we won't ever have to slow down long enough to face what is going on inside of us. Sadly, as we re-invent ourselves spiritually every one or two generations, we think we've done something astounding when in fact our "new" spiritual systems tend to be like each exciting new automobile that was released in the 1950s and 1960s—flashy superficial changes like tailfins but the same old car inside. What is inside of us won't go away, and it can't really be covered up very well, either. And so we lose our appreciation for life itself as we seek newer and newer "spiritual" highs in the forms of automobile tailfins and new belief systems.

A BLESSING IN COUNTY TIPPERARY

We were working in Ireland a few years ago and were blessed with a beautiful experience. It was something we had experienced over and over before, but this time it was just different enough to make it eternally memorable. At the end of a long day of presenting difficult information about painful families, we did a concluding exercise in which everyone wrote down three little things that they liked. In America it might be things like fine-tipped pens, playing with a puppy, walking on the beach at night with your lover, a good book, a well-organized hard-disc on your computer or the sound of a Harley-Davidson roaring down the open road. It is such a simple exercise and yet over the years we have seen groups of physicians and attorneys, truck drivers and nurses, social workers and business executives weep openly as each man and woman nervously but proudly reads his or her list while everyone else quietly listens. The things we appreciate say more about us than almost anything else, which is why we ask our audiences to listen respectfully, read their list and not explain or defend what they share. What we like, want, or appreciate needs no defense or justification. It is who we are. The list is simply a matter of preference. Read the three items on your list and then pass.

When it happens this way—with reverence, attention and care—it is nearly impossible not to be moved deeply as each person reads her or his list. It creates a safe but vulnerable atmosphere that allows each human being in the room to be proud of his uniqueness while appreciating and connecting with everyone else. This gives each man and woman in the room the chance to briefly experience the magic paradox of simultaneous separateness and togetherness. I am unique so no one will ever understand me, but I can see myself in your soul so I will never be alone.

And so around the room they went, each person nervously awaiting her turn to read her list, each person warmly receiving the list of his fellows. We were tired. One of us had been sick for several days and was ready to rest. It was our first visit to Ireland. We had ancestors here. It was a homecoming, but we were working and, therefore, had to present our material as professionally as we could. We worried about how we would be received, because an American speaker the year before had not been well-received. As the long day slowly came to a close with each person reading the items on his list, it appeared that we had connected with an ancestry we had only read about in books. We shared pain and joy with people we worried might not like us, and we formed an intimate bond with a marvelous group of human beings from another country. As the 85th person read the three items on his list, we felt tears running down our cheeks, and then we looked up and saw tears running down the cheeks of 85 people. All of us had been deeply moved by the experience, which turned out to be the perfect ending to a memorable day.

THE LITTLE THINGS

What did members of our Irish audience like? They mentioned things like fine-tipped pens, playing with a puppy, walking along the edge of the sea with a lover, a good book, quietly fishing on a nearby lake, sitting by a warm fire on a chilly night, the smell of fresh coffee brewing in the morning, big puffy clouds, rain, hugs, children, jogging, quaint little shops, a good heated discussion, movies, sailing, a clean house, a down comforter, horses, good friends, sex, French pastries . . . you know, typical little things that make us happy.

One of life's most pleasant experiences can be to share an afternoon walk with a good friend, especially if we have spent the majority of our life being lonely. The smell of fresh air to a man just released from prison can be the closest thing to heaven on earth. The warmth of the early summer sunlight penetrating one's skin can be euphoric, especially if it comes after a long, cold winter.

Sometimes we have to experience the depths of deprivation before we can truly appreciate the important things in life—the little things. One of the deepest joys of being psychologists is that we are often allowed to witness someone's transformation from unappreciative and addictive to appreciative and spiritual. It's not that we should intentionally deprive ourselves or set out to ruin our lives in the hopes that we will someday be able to appreciate life's subtleties. It's just that when we are not medicating ourselves with addictive or compulsive behaviors, life presents us with enough natural pain and deprivation that eventually we can be grateful for the little things that count so much, but only if we grow up.

IDENTITY, SPIRITUALITY AND PLEASURE

Knowing what pleases us is a crucial piece of identity and spirituality. If you have the opportunity to visit someone who is suffering from untreated depression, you may catch a glimpse of what we mean. This person's surroundings will often reflect his mental state. You may notice few pictures on the walls, no flowers or decorations around the house, no expressions of self to be found anywhere. If these things are present, you might notice that the home has not been cared for lately, as if the person living there is from out of town and on business, with little time to make a home out of his house. What we like, what we want and how we express our inner selves in our living spaces are essential aspects of soulfulness. In many unhealthy families, little attention is paid to aesthetics and even less to the individual desires of each family member. A child wants her room painted a certain color, but her parents don't listen to her wishes. Mom buys five dollars-worth of flowers to decorate the table, and Dad explodes as if she'd just purchased the Taj Mahal. In healthier families, each person's identity and spirit are viewed as gifts from creation that are to be revered and nurtured for the betterment of the whole system. When one child likes a different color than the rest, it is accepted and appreciated as an expression of her individual will. Willfulness is seen as a sign of spirit and identity, not as a sign of impudence and defiance. An infant spies a rattle in her crib, and her heart leaps with excitement as she reaches out her tiny hand to grasp it. She isn't just picking up a toy. She is casting her spirit out into the universe so that it can learn and deepen and expand. A man decorates his new apartment, and in doing so he expresses, reinforces and clarifies his identity and his spirit. As we learn what pleases us, as we reach out into creation to feel all that is out there, our inner selves deepen and bloom. When we don't know what we like, and when we never experience what pleases us, it is a clear sign that something is hurting inside.

APPRECIATION IN RELATIONSHIPS

It is often said that the things we appreciate about each other also contain the seeds of our discontent. A man says that it drives him crazy that his partner is so fussy about their home, but in the next breath he compliments her on what a good housekeeper she is. A woman complains that her partner is too rational, but she admires him for his successful law career. Appreciation is a complex act, and it increases in depth and simplicity as we deepen.

In working with couples, we ask each of the partners to take a closer look at what they appreciate about each other and then we have them practice sharing these things directly. It sounds like such a simple task that should be much easier than telling your partner what makes you angry, but it's actually just as risky. Whenever we expose our vulnerability to another human being, there is the risk of getting hurt; and it is surely an act of vulnerability to tell someone that we love them dearly and would be miserable without them. It exposes our healthy interdependency.

It is a wonderful exercise and typically fills our consultation room with warmth, acceptance and delight. It is sheer joy for us to hear a man tell his wife that he values her more than anything else in the world and that he appreciates all that she does, all that she is, how much she graces his life and what a good friend she has become to him. He says he appreciates her extroversion, how she can go out into the world and meet people and make things happen. He appreciates her smile, her sense of humor, her sensitivity to others' feelings, her ability to stand up to him when she feels she needs to, and her sexiness. A woman tells her husband that she appreciates his strength, his know-how and worldliness, his reflective spirit that balances her extroverted one, his depth, his sense of humor—she has always liked that—and his power and his gentleness. She doesn't like weak, passive men, she says, and he's no weak, passive man.

Many couples tell us that with regularity one will spontaneously turn to the other and say, "I really love you and appreciate you." The other will bask in the comment and then later will spontaneously say the same kind of thing in return. They don't do this because they read it in a book or because they were told to do it in a workshop. They feel it and mean it because they have suffered life's disappointments and accept what life has to offer, and because they know how fragile life is and how dear a moment can be.

A man told us how he used to belittle people who appreciated things, especially if they were the simple things in life that enrich us so much. He was a bit like Ebeneezer Scrooge in that regard. Everything was a humbug. Adults who enjoyed playing with puppies were especially "humbugful," as were reading the comics in the newspaper on Sunday morning, spy novels, dreaming about the future and holding hands while walking through the park. "How embarrassing for them," he would mutter under his breath. "Grown adults holding hands. How corny." "Who cares what color car you have," he would pronounce. "A car is a means of transporting oneself from point A to point B. Just buy the damned thing and let's get out of here," he would mumble in disgust. And then he began to lose things. First, he lost a good friend who simply couldn't bear to be around all of the negativity and criticism. Then he lost a lung to cancer. Then his mother died, and then his father. Then his wife divorced him because he was so miserable to live with. He was almost killed in an automobile accident, and endured a painful and protracted recovery.

Life had brought him not just to his knees but to death's very door. As he stood at the threshold, he realized for the first time that there is no discernible difference between life and death—they are the same—and for the first time in his life he was able to appreciate the little things in life. He said, "I used to approach life as if it were an all-you-can-eat restaurant. I'd pile on the mashed potatoes and gravy and slosh it all down with a pitcher of beer, not caring how it tasted or the amount of care that had gone into preparing it. Now it's more like a delicately prepared and presented Japanese or French meal in which the portions are much smaller, great time and effort have been put into creating it for me, and the soul-sustaining subtleties of taste and texture are as important as the practical, life-sustaining calories and nutrients in the meal." One day many years later he was talking about his second marriage and he said with simplicity and sincerity, "This relationship is so good. There are days when I wake up and have to think twice to make sure I'm not in a fantasy. I am so grateful for this person who sleeps next to me every night. I am grateful for our passion, for our fights, for our laughter, for our tears, and for all the trivial, silly little things that we enjoy together. I never could have appreciated these things ten years ago. I finally have a glimpse of what life is really about."

An old man suffers a stroke and spends his last five years of life nearly bedridden after 75 years of being active, driven and goal-oriented. Is it a cruel trick or a subtle gift that life has brought to him? Punishment for past sins or a sacred opportunity to fill in the hidden corners of his soul that had been overlooked during his busy life? A woman lives with dependency fears all of her life and then spends the last five years of her husband's life in terror that he might die and she might be alone forever. When he dies, she grieves, and then she has peace in her life despite the fact that she is alone. She had to experience the one thing she feared the most before she was able to live with dignity.

We have worked with Americans, Mexicans, Canadians, British, Irish, South Africans, Japanese, Chinese, French, Norwegians, Swedish, Germans and many more. And the list of little things that human beings like goes on . . . the crunch of snow beneath your boots on a freezing, moonlit night, flannel underwear, hummingbirds, Chardonnay, Paris at night, the Kohala Coast of Hawaii, dry desert air, Elton John's music, a wild summer thunderstorm, mountain streams, lots of fresh ground pepper on my salad, a child's laughter, swimming in icy water, my cat, clean teeth, just the right make-up, sensual sex on a warm afternoon, a good play, Bangkok, soft skin, chocolate, Persian rugs, the *Los Angeles Times* on Sunday morning, Labrador retrievers, hardwood floors, fresh sheets, oranges, a symphony orchestra . . .

Chapter 18

INTEGRITY, HONOR AND ACCOUNTABILITY

Honor and shame from no condition rise; Act well your part, there all the honor lies.

Alexander Pope
An Essay On Man, 1734

We are hungry for basic virtues. After years of unrestrained economic growth and materialism followed by the painful realities of multiple recessions and stagnations, we finally seem to be swinging back to some kind of national balance, at least in what we long for. This explains why William Bennett's *The Book of Virtues* was such a huge bestseller. Because of the moral confusion that results from rapid social change, it is good to stop and reflect on the basic values that form the foundation of any civilized nation and to look for examples of integrity and honor among the citizens of this great planet of ours. Because despite our complaints to the contrary, there are innumerable examples of fine men and women who to this day exhibit integrity, honor and accountability.

When we think of integrity and honor, Mother Theresa immediately comes to mind, as do Nelson Mandela, Rosa Parks, Abraham Lincoln and Andrei Sakharov. Surprisingly, even the ranks of contemporary politicians are not devoid of figures who have displayed tremendous integrity. Jimmy and Rosalynn Carter didn't just preach about the value of moral leadership while they were in The White House, they actually lived it. Like George Washington who returned to his farm rather than being pronounced king by an adoring America, the Carters have returned to the earth through Habitat for Humanity. Working with their hands to build houses for and with the poor, they also bring together people from across the socioeconomic and racial spectrum. How easy it would be for the Carters to cash in on the presidency and then live in the lap of luxury for the rest of their years. And how extraordinary for a former president and first lady of the United States to do such "lowly" work. They are surely the finest of people.

There is Elliott Richardson, attorney general under Richard Nixon, who made the earth-shattering and politically unheard-of decision to resign rather than fire Special Prosecutor Archibald Cox as he had been ordered to do by the Nixon administration. Many years later it is easy to say, "Well, of course, he resigned. Wouldn't anybody have done the same?" But the fact is that very few people have ever shown that kind of moral courage under such intense public scrutiny. The Watergate scandal was still a mass of confusion, nobody really knew the truth, and as far as Elliott Richardson knew, he was committing political suicide when he resigned, but he did it anyway. We admire him profoundly for it.

WHAT ARE INTEGRITY AND HONOR?

Integrity and honor mean many things. The words strike several chords as they reverberate inside of our souls. They mean being consistent and trustworthy, having values that are on a higher plane than simply serving the self, and they include honesty, fairness and wholeness. These are lofty ideals, and it is, therefore, important to keep in mind that no one is perfect and that each individual defines these terms differently. Being consistent and trustworthy does not necessarily mean being punctual, although it might include that under certain circumstances.

A woman has the habit of being 30 minutes late for most of her social and work engagements yet she is honest and true and fair in her dealings with people. It is a minor annoying quirk that occasionally causes problems for those around her, but it does not permeate the rest of her life or behavior and thus would not be a threat to the integrity of her intimacy with others. But what if she were late all the time, sometimes for over an hour or two, and what if that was just the tip of the iceberg in terms of her respect for others' feelings? What if she were always late, rarely followed through with the commitments she made, never acknowledged how her behavior affected others and tended to blame others for being "too rigid?" Then we would speak of her lacking integrity.

Sometimes people confuse things like punctuality and rule-following with integrity and honor. For example, a man is always on time, always tries to be nice to others, remembers birthdays and anniversaries, hardly ever raises his voice in anger, reads the Bible, espouses virtue and honor, and is liked by most of his associates. And then one day there is a conflict at work or home that requires him to act by taking a clear position on a difficult issue, but he finds himself unable to do it. He knows what his stated values are, and everyone else knows what they are, too;

but he can't respond when the chips are down. We might then question his integrity when it comes to those particular values because he lacks consistency between what he says and what he does. We recall the words of a Sufi master who said, "I no longer listen to what people say. I watch what they do." Being trustworthy and consistent in our values requires that we not just verbalize but also act according to those words. Some of the most eloquent conceptualizers and orators have very little integrity and honor when it comes to their own behavior.

At the same time, it is important to leave room for one's humanity. A man may have impeccable integrity when it comes to his professional life but have a deep flaw in his character somewhere else. He might be another Elliott Richardson or Nelson Mandela at work but have difficulty living according to his higher values in his marriage. Do we judge him as lacking integrity altogether, or can we make room in our hearts and minds to honor his strength and courage at work despite his personal flaws? Was Winston Churchill an alcoholic, cigar-smoking tyrant, or was he a tremendously courageous leader who helped to save the free world? Some would focus on the former, but we hope most would focus on the latter.

As qualities of adulthood, integrity and honor are always developing, always in process, always deepening. A woman may live a life of quiet desperation and victimhood in which she sacrifices her integrity year after year for the sake of family unity, and then late in her life she may suddenly take a courageous stand on a powerful issue. In that one courageous act, she may erase an entire lifetime of moral equivocation so that her life has as much meaning as her death. It is never too late to choose wholeness over fragmentation if only we can muster the courage to do it. In *Richard II*, Shakespeare wrote, "Mine honor is my life; both grow in one; Take honor from me and my life is done."

ACCOUNTABILITY

When you want to know where your resources are, how they have been utilized, how much you have left and how much you need in the future, you might hire an accountant to help you. Although we sometimes joke about creative accounting, the "accountant jokes" usually center on the sharp pencil used by the accountant and the fact that every penny must be accounted for when doing a formal audit—which explains why we nickname them "bean counters." When we move into the murky realm of human relationships, it is even harder to do an accurate accounting, because feelings and behaviors are less quantifiable than dollars and cents. But we must try. Accountability is a crucial aspect of integrity and honor.

A woman is miserable in her marriage and then suddenly finds herself falling in love with another man. She is so lonely and empty in her marriage and so afraid of disturbing the painful balance between herself, her husband and her children, that she convinces herself to accept the affair as the lesser of two evils—divorce being the other. As she gets more deeply embroiled in the affair, it becomes harder and harder to juggle both relationships until one day the whole delicately balanced house of cards comes crashing down around her. She looks into the frightened eyes of her husband who has just asked her point-blank if she is having an affair. As she says "yes," she realizes that the greatest damage that she has done to him is to lie when she knew that he suspected something all along, because it deprived him of the dignity of being able to respond to reality.

We all weave tangled webs within the structure of our lives now and then, and many people fall into extramarital affairs without seeming to know how it happened. The critical question is, "How do we handle our relationship pain in the future once we have seen and felt the terrible damage caused by this kind of deceit?" A woman who is open to the deepening of integrity and honor within her soul will take the huge risk to do a personal accounting of the experience. Her first action after doing this might be to apologize, without excuses, for interfering with her husband's reality and therefore his dignity. She might wait patiently as he expresses his shock, his outrage, his deep hurt, his betrayal and his fears. Owning up to the affair levels the playing field just as keeping it secret gives her more power than is fair. Once it is out in the open, she might also act honorably by either ending the marriage if she feels it is hopeless, or by ending the affair so that she can work on the marriage and give it another chance, unfettered by the intrusion of the other relationship.

Regardless of what happens to her marriage, if this woman is becoming truly accountable and honorable, she will no longer be free to choose a hidden affair as an indirect way of dealing with relationship pain in the future. It simply won't be an option any longer, because she knows from firsthand experience how much destruction it causes. As our clients move towards accountability, we liken it to being in a room with doors in each corner, and they paint themselves into the corner of their own choosing. If it is an accountable choice, they will paint themselves into the corner where the door opens up to honesty and directness in relationships. Their only available choice will be to resolve the disappointment and unhappiness in their current relationship, cleanly and respectfully, before moving on to another relationship.

An adult man, in this case, can weather the end of even the deepest of relationships, because he knows that life is filled with endings. It is the lack of consistency, honesty and integrity that makes him feel so crazy. And it is the lack of accountability that keeps him stuck in the old, painful relationship. A grown-up man can come to accept that his relationship is over if his partner is forthright and clear about what is in her heart. When she maintains her false dignity by not being honest then he must struggle with the disrespect implied by her lack of honesty—a struggle that is harder to release.

Accountability does not mean that we continually beat ourselves up for all of our limitations. We help people see that their defenses and addictions developed as a way to protect themselves from painful circumstances when they were children, and that, as children, they did not have the power to protect themselves in healthy ways. This allows the person to have self-acceptance and forgiveness so that he can work through the shame of his limitations. But as Southern California therapist Lyndel Brennan notes, self-acceptance or acceptance of another's limitations does not mean that we condone those limitations. We can forgive another's hurting us, but we can also expect them to work on their problems so that they stop the hurt.

CULTIVATING INTEGRITY, HONOR AND ACCOUNTABILITY

Jean Piaget wrote that children learn empathy more while playing in the sandbox than from being told to memorize rules. By this, we believe he meant that as we struggle with each other we directly experience the impact of our behavior on others—and theirs on us. I take your toy away from you and laugh at your tears, and then a bigger or faster child takes my toy away from me and I cry. I lie about my commitment to you and it violate your trust, and then another person lies about his commitment to me and violates my trust. These experiences can *then* be plugged into the moral teachings of our greater society so that we no longer behave respectfully just because the law says we must—we do so because of our deepened empathy and understanding of the reasons underlying the law.

Does this mean that I must kill someone before I can understand why killing is wrong? Of course not. Life experiences are generalizable and the human mind is perfectly capable of extrapolating from a less severe example to a more severe one. If someone beats me with words and attempts to kill my spirit with emotional neglect, can I not get a strong feeling for what it must be like to be beaten with a pipe and have my life taken from me?

We believe that each human being, no matter how much he hurts later, is born with an empathic/ethical drive. This may sound like a pipe dream given the violence in our society today, but we don't think so. We have seen what appeared to be incorrigible offenders eventually reclaim their dignity by becoming accountable. We have seen people who were so driven by their sexuality that they never thought they could maintain a sexually monogamous relationship with their partner, but they have. Accountability is a choice. It is an attribute of the soul that can be cultivated. And while being accountable means that we lose certain "freedoms," it also means that we gain immeasurable gifts along the way, which is why it is worth pursuing.

It is essential to respect the truth that integrity, honor and accountability begin in our homes and then spread past those four walls into the world beyond. A little boy overhears his mother say to his father, "You hurt my feelings when you said that, and I didn't like it." Then he hears his father say, "You're right. I'm sorry. I was out of line with that comment." Day in and day out, year after year, this little boy sees and hears his parents sticking up for themselves, fighting with clarity and respect, owning up to their faults without trying to weasel out of them, giving each other room to make mistakes without always being taken to task, taking risks, acting on their values rather than just talking about them, appreciating and loving each other, and enjoying their relationship. When this little boy becomes a man, he automatically conducts the majority of his life with integrity and honor.

For those of us who lacked good examples of accountability when we were growing up, cultivating integrity and honor begins with our fearless assessment of who we are and how we affect other human beings. Sometimes life invites us to do such an accounting and sometimes life grabs us by the throat and demands that we do it, as in the case of the man who went to prison for unintentionally killing another man in a drunken bar fight. He struggled and fought fiercely and bitterly for many years, angry at those who had imprisoned him, and even angrier beneath it all at those who hurt him when he was little. The angrier he became the less anyone was willing to consider his parole, until one day at the age of 42 he simply surrendered. He entered the prison's alcohol rehabilitation program for the third time, but this time he did it voluntarily, not because his spirit was broken but because it finally demanded a voice—it had finally come to life after being dormant all those years.

Upon completing the program, he initiated a systematic process of becoming accountable to those he had hurt throughout his life. Without any court's suggestion or request, he began to make restitution or wrote contracts for restitution that he pledged to fulfill upon gaining his freedom and getting a job. The pledges were to himself alone. No one else knew about them. Upon his release from prison, he came to see us to help maintain his accountable behavior and to heal all of the old wounds that had accumulated from his painful childhood. He was a remarkable man, as close to a saint as we had ever personally encountered.

After two years of intermittent work with us, he came in for a session carrying several pieces of yellowed, creased old paper. He explained that these were the pledges of restitution he had written in prison, that he had shared them with no one and that he had been living in near-poverty because he was putting money away and volunteering his services to make good on the pledges. He had brought them in to formally honor the people he had hurt and to share his actions with us so that we could privately bear witness to what he had done, allowing his soul to rest at last. Our office was filled with warmth and light and tears, and a depth of dignity and honor that we have not felt since then. He knew that this had to be a private gesture, because he had passed very profoundly through this door to the soul of adulthood.

Chapter 19

TRADITION, STRUCTURE AND DISCIPLINE

It is a reverend thing to see an ancient castle or building not in decay: or to see a fair timber tree sound and perfect. How much more to behold an ancient and noble family which hath stood against the waves and weathers of time.

Francis Bacon
Essays, 1625

TRADITION AND HISTORY

Adults are disciplined and their lives are structured. They value tradition, because it grounds them within the larger context of human history and thus provides a meaning system that is stable in the face of life's inevitable instabilities. Even rituals and traditions that seem outdated in our technocratic societies have value, as evidenced by Britain's royalty. Whenever the debate is renewed about whether to end such a costly and seemingly useless British institution, wiser heads prevail, and not just because the monarchy is a prime tourist attraction. There is a different feel to England that comes from the people's pride in their history and in their traditions. There is a structure to English society that some would label repressive, although it could also be called respectful. There is still a feeling of safety and boundary in

London, a city of 8 million people, that we have not experienced in any large city in the United States.

Some people dismiss tradition and rootedness as being too confining or meaningless in such a fast-moving society. Some of us feel like our traditional institutions and belief systems are archaic. Some of us act as if our family history ends with our parents or grandparents. And some of us believe that history itself doesn't matter because in America we have limitless potential to create and recreate our own futures. But in 80 B.C. Cicero wrote, "Not to know what happened before one was born is always to be a child." Each of us has a childhood history and whether we acknowledge it or not, each of us also has a family and cultural history that extends well beyond our grandparents. To ignore or deny our history and traditions is to relegate a part of our souls to perpetual immaturity.

A DISTURBING VAGUENESS

A man came to us complaining of a disturbing vagueness in his life. He was a pleasant person who got along well with others, but he longed for something in his life that he could not describe. He talked at length about his childhood, which on the surface appeared clinically unremarkable. There was no physical abuse, no sexual abuse, no divorce, no alcoholism, no overt trauma, no deaths, no major losses. He spoke warmly of his parents and siblings, said that he did well in school, talked about having many friends and described a career path that seemed typical of someone his age. The more he talked about his life the more confused he became, because nothing stood out to help explain his uncomfortable feelings.

We began by simply exploring with him the ways in which he experienced this vagueness that haunted him, encouraging him to put as many words on the experience as he could. With great difficulty at first, he struggled to find those words, which slowly emerged from deep within his soul: "Uneasy." "Disconnected." "Confused." "Floundering." "Aimless." "Not grounded." "Ethereal." "Drifting." "Shallow." "Vague." "Detached." "Rootless." "Uncommitted." As each word took form and entered the room, we noticed subtle changes in his voice and facial expression indicating increased energy and connectedness with self. He finally blurted out, "What the hell is going on? My childhood was perfect! I have everything anyone could ever want!" We quickly asked, "There's something more. What else do you want?" He quickly replied, "Meaning! And roots!"

At last he had a handle to grasp. As we explored what these words meant to him, clear patterns slowly began to emerge. During our initial family history with this man, we had noticed that his descriptions of his grandparents and other family lineage were very vague, and now it was time to fit that observation in with his recent emotional discovery. It turned out that his maternal grandfather was a Jewish man from Poland and his maternal grandmother was a Catholic woman from France. They had such tumultuous conflicts over religion throughout his mother's childhood that by the time she married his father, she had vowed not to let religion be an issue in her marriage or in her children's lives. This man's paternal grandfather had failed at a business back in Europe and had later developed chronic depression after coming to America and marrying. His grandfather's depression was a matter of family shame that became buried in secrecy. At the same time, religion was not an integral part of their family, which his mother found very appealing. Mom saw Dad as a man with whom religious conflict would not be an issue. Her marriage to him would represent an end to the religious pain she had endured as a child.

And so his parents struck an unconscious bargain not to let religion get in their way and not to talk about the depression in Dad's family. Mom and Dad rarely talked about their parents, choosing instead to move forward and become fully assimilated into suburban American culture. Like many early Americans who came here to start over completely, leaving their past and their roots behind, this man's parents embraced the future and left their own pasts behind. They attended a small Methodist church irregularly and prided themselves in their flexible approach to religion and religious dogma. They read books on proper childrearing techniques, attended their children's school plays and football games, helped with homework, included their children in family chores and voted in every national election.

As we delved into these patterns with this man, he began to form a clear picture in his mind of what had been missing in his life. He wasn't angry about it. In fact, he was appropriately grateful for the many wonderful things his parents had done for him and his siblings. But he realized that he actually envied people who had deep values and commitments, and that he longed for these himself. We asked him to create a collage that would be an expression of his inner longings, and the result was startling in its clarity. He chose to cut out pictures and words from magazines and paste them onto a three-foot square piece of tagboard. He explained that he had begun by cutting out every word and picture that caught his eye without stopping to analyze its significance, which we acknowledged was a good way to connect with his unconscious. He spread these dozens of symbols across the floor of his spare bedroom and let them lay there for several days so that he could peek in whenever the spirit moved him and simply absorb what his unconscious had selected.

With great animation, he shared the gradual sorting and selection process that took place in the back of his mind over the next few weeks. One night he dreamed about the collage. It entered his mind one day while he was at work. He thought about it as he drove home one day. He began to sort the items into groups, and then he sorted the groups into those he would keep and those he would not. Six weeks after we gave him the assignment, he brought in the completed creation. It was elegant in its simplicity. As our eyes scanned back and forth across his collage, the most notable image was a large picture of St. Patrick's Cathedral. Nearby, and almost as salient, was a picture of a symphony orchestra with the Mona Lisa overlapping its outer edges. We kept scanning and processing the symbols and meanings in his collage as we simultaneously scanned and processed all that we had learned about this man during our previous sessions. As we abstracted a coherent picture from the thousands of facts then at hand, two themes were indisputably apparent. This man clearly had a deep longing for religion and culture.

The energy released by his inner soul-searching was now free to be focused and directed. He no longer felt vague and empty. He now felt a hunger for life that filled his spirit with an excitement and anticipation that led him to tour Europe and explore his cultural roots, take classes in art and music appreciation, and eventually study and value both Judaism and Catholicism with incredible depth. A few years after he completed his work with us, we received a letter from this man which said in part, "I have gained an appreciation for the pain and shame surrounding the depression in my family . . . and I am still struggling with whether I want to practice Judaism or Catholicism because they both have such beautiful, rich traditions and deep systems of meaning. That I have come to engage the struggle, to ask the questions, to embrace some of those values is most important right now. I am finally alive."

THE DEVELOPMENT OF STRUCTURE

Without some structure, life is chaos. As we grow up, it is the structure provided for us by our parents that creates the safety needed for our exploration of the larger world outside. A young child goes about his busy day unconsciously trusting that someone is in charge. He gets very tired and cranky at night, but a part of him says he should stay up so he won't miss any of the fun. Safe parents will put him to bed at his bedtime, because they know he needs the sleep, and because they know he needs the structure. And so he goes to bed and awakens the next day rested, and still unconsciously trusting that someone is in charge. This structure becomes internalized over the years—it becomes a part of the child deep inside—so that by the time he reaches adulthood he is able to structure his own life without outside help. He then has the ability to be responsible, competent and happy. Internal structure and discipline are two of the greatest gifts we can give our children.

TRADITION, STRUCTURE AND DISCIPLINE

Janis Joplin, the 1960s rock singer whose consumptive lifestyle eventually killed her, sang angrily, sadly and powerfully that "freedom" was the same as having nothing left to lose. These alienated words reflected the deep pain that she must have been feeling and symbolized the tragic mindset that resulted in her untimely death. Some people confuse tradition, structure and discipline with compulsivity and lack of freedom. They are very different. Inflexible adherence to rules is compulsive, but unlimited defiance of healthy structure is sociopathic. Neither extreme is good.

Discipline, on the other hand, is the foundation of soulful living. An undisciplined artist is unable to bring his creativity to fruition. An undisciplined scientist is unable to make useful sense of his discoveries. Undisciplined love is childish, neurotic and continually painful. An undisciplined society is unsafe. While the rigid, soul-less practice of traditions is an empty exercise, a life without traditions is also empty because our traditions and institutions bind us to each other and to our collective history. There is great wisdom in those who believe that true freedom carries with it the welcome requirement of responsibility. If freedom *is* just another word for nothing left to lose, then we are surely lost.

People who live in democratic societies have many freedoms. We have the freedom to criticize our leaders, the freedom to explore our unconscious depths, the freedom to come and go as we please, and the freedom to say what we choose. If we don't like the leader we have elected, we can elect a new one. If we don't like the religion in which we were raised, we can start a new one. But we can carry this notion of freedom too far. We hear from many people who have tried to correct past wrongs done to them by rejecting established institutions and beliefs wholeheartedly, only to find that their new belief systems are shallow and unfulfilling. A woman leaves the church of her childhood because of its rigid dogma and swings to the other extreme in which she embraces a vague spiritualism that ultimately has no meaning for her. A man stops voting because he believes that all government is bad, thereby giving up any chance that he might influence the direction of his government in the future.

Undisciplined, unorganized beliefs tend to be diffuse, vague and unsatisfying. It is a fact of human nature that when we are unhappy with our situation anything new looks better at first, which is why we say "the grass is always greener on the other side of the fence." But an adult is able to wait and see, withholding final judgment until he has enough evidence to make a meaningful choice. And so the woman who dabbles in New Age spiritualism may be enriched by the experience as she takes the deepening she has gained from it and returns to a more traditional religion. And the man who doesn't vote in a few elections may thereby purge his disgust with government, allowing him to get back into the exciting fray of daily life among other humans, which is called politics.

As we grow and mature we internalize the limits, structure and traditions that were provided for us as children. We connect with relatives and friends and hear stories about our family's roots so that we gradually understand the patterns and nuances of life in our families and within ourselves. We become involved in our cultural institutions and learn about our collective history so that we can have wisdom. We learn the importance of art and music as symbols of our cultures and as expressions of the deepest parts of ourselves. We come to value law not because of what it prevents us from doing, but because of the deeper freedoms afforded to us by the structure and safety created by law. We value self-discipline, because we learn how much more deeply we can live with it, than without it.

At each stage of adulthood, we reach back through the previous years and sift through what we find, each time gaining more complexity and depth, and paradoxically, each time gaining more simplicity and elegance in how we live our lives. We tie up loose ends that may still be perplexing, and then we reach back even farther to gather up the strands of meaning and connection with past generations and with our culture as a whole, eventually organizing the whole into a structure more meaningful than before. This is not a lock-step, linear process by any means, and it is never completely finished. But it is what adulthood is all about.

The ability to honor and care for our established institutions and traditions, to value the structure within us as well as in society at large, and to nurture self-discipline in our daily lives is what allows us to pass through the doors to adulthood with safety, reverence and respect.

Chapter 20

FAITH, HOPE AND SPIRITUALITY

Faith has to do with things that are not seen, and hope with things that are not in hand.

Thomas Aquinas
Summa Theologiae, c. 1265

Adults are able to embrace the spirituality that is inherent in all human beings. This means that part of being grown up is the ability to struggle with, appreciate, explore and wonder about the unexplainable in the universe. It also means the willingness to have a relationship with something beyond ourselves and to admit that we cannot control everything—the ability to surrender now and then. Being spiritual does not necessarily mean that we belong to an organized religion, nor does it in any way exclude those who are religious.

THE FOUNDATIONS OF HOPE

Because one of our previous books was devoted entirely to spirituality, we would like to focus on just one aspect of it: the role of hope and faith in maintaining emotional stability throughout a typical lifetime that is punctuated by sorrows as well as joys. In other words, how does one person endure heartache, tragedy or loss, and do it with grace, dignity and deepening of the soul? And why does another person experience the same losses or tragedies and not fare so well? Many years ago we read an article by the world-renowned developmental psychologist Urie Bronfenbrenner of Cornell University in which he stated that those who eventually bounced back from great trauma or tragedy in childhood had at least one person in life who was crazy about them. It was a startlingly down-to-earth synopsis from such a distinguished scientist, and we have not forgotten it.

"One person in your life who is just plain crazy about you." It's a fascinating thought upon which to reflect. It could mean an aunt or uncle who cared deeply for you despite the neglect or abuse you experienced at home. It could be a mother or father who took seriously the job of parenting despite the neglect of the other parent. It could be a family friend, a therapist, a minister or priest, or a coach or teacher. One person in your life who is just plain crazy about you. It's so simple.

It also fits quite well into Erik Erikson's thoughts about the first stage of life, in which we struggle with trust vs. mistrust. The developmental task of an infant is to get a sense that she will endure despite the intermittent pain and unpredictability that life brings. This is accomplished if the infant is fed, diapered, held and generally cared for in predictable ways. But it also requires that the infant gradually experiences small doses of discomfort and unpredictability so that she can learn that life works out even when she doesn't always get what she wants. Interestingly, Erikson felt that the underlying strength that developed during this stage was hope, about which John Keats wrote: "Sweet hope, ethereal balm upon me shed, And wave thy silver pinions o'er my head."

LIFE'S RHYTHMS

Some people try to control every aspect of life, but it is a losing battle. Life isn't really cruel as much as it is bigger than us and therefore seems cruel at times, especially when it doesn't go the way we planned. A woman dreams of having grandchildren but never does. A man wants to become a lawyer but doesn't get admitted to law school. We want to go to the beach on Saturday but it rains all day. There are just too many variables in life that we can't control. But amidst all of the unpredictability in life there is also plenty that we can control. Control is not all bad. We build houses to protect ourselves from inclement weather, and most of the time they function that way. We research the automobile market and select a car with a good repair record and are usually rewarded for the effort by owning a car that requires little maintenance.

A distinct advantage of growing up in a fairly healthy family is that the day-in and day-out of living together and experiencing life's ups and downs in a boundaried, supportive environment allows us to internalize life's rhythms. Being in a family is a hypnotic process—we learn mostly by being in it and absorbing what is there rather than by direct teaching. A fire destroys part of our house, and although we are frightened and our sense of trust is betrayed, we experience our family rebounding, rebuilding and continuing. Someone gets seriously ill, and we watch as the family moves through it together. We fall in love as teenagers, fall out of love, find understanding and warmth from our family, learn from it and then go forward. People fight, hate each other for a moment, have conflict, resolve it and love each other again.

Nature is filled with patterns and rhythms, from the swells that sweep across our vast oceans, to the formation and evaporation of storm clouds, to the continual changing of the seasons. Life begins, endures for a time and then ends, only to be replaced by new life. People who are filled with hope have accepted and embraced these rhythms. People who lack hope and faith fight with them, try to control them and despair in the disappointment that comes with being unable to do so. Without hope it is as if we have no memory of past rhythms, so that when fall begins we are irreparably crushed like the dry leaves drifting to the ground on a cold October afternoon.

The patience that comes with acknowledging life's rhythms can come most serendipitously. A woman told us that one day she learned a great lesson from watching her dog. The woman was struggling with her need to control everything and with her impatience when life did not go exactly as she had planned. One afternoon she was so frustrated that she didn't want to try any longer. So she just sat and watched her dog. Her dog sat and watched her. She knew the dog probably wanted to play because the dog always wanted to play, but she didn't have the energy. She watched the dog some more. The dog looked up. The dog put his head down, resting his head on his paws. The woman thought the dog had lost interest, but whenever she moved she could see the dog's eyes following her. She just knew the dog wanted to play. And then it dawned on her—the dog had patience. The dog somehow knew that sooner or later life would provide. The woman was so thankful and excited for what the dog had taught her that she jumped to her feet, put on her running clothes, yelled for the dog to follow her and then took her dog to the park to play. The woman was ecstatic, as was her dog.

In *Translating LA*, a magically crafted, loving, yet realistic portrait of our most enigmatic city, Peter Theroux described the aftermath of the triple tragedies of a terrible riot followed by two huge earthquakes: "And yet here we all were. The city was once again being repaired and prepared, and the gentle weather seemed to promise that God had not meant it after all." For all of its glitter, narcissism and transience, and despite our bemused contempt for this City of Angels, the people of Los Angeles represent a striking and constant reminder that life is bigger than any one of us, and that the human spirit is indeed indomitable. The collision of the rhythms of nature and the rhythms of cultures proceeds whether we like it or not; tearing down, building up, creating and re-creating. It isn't just life that goes on. Even life in Los Angeles goes on.

And so it is that trust springs from care, and hope continually pushes up from the fertile ground of trust. An adult with a basic sense of trust will embrace the rhythms of life and will come to appreciate them even when they are in a down-cycle. While acknowledging her fear of death and loneliness, she will not be held hostage by those fears. Rather, she will be deepened by them.

FEAR, CONTROL, HOPE, FAITH AND SPIRITUALITY

People sometimes forget the simple relationship between fear and control. Whenever we try to control something, there is always a subtle element of fear involved. A man gets angry and tries to make his partner hurry up so they won't be late for a concert, because he is afraid they will miss the beginning. A woman reinforces the foundation of her house, because she is afraid of earthquake damage. A little boy hides his favorite toy, because he is afraid his sister will take it when he is outside playing. A man batters his wife, because he is afraid if he stops controlling her, she will leave him. No matter what the circumstance, when we try to control something or someone, there is always at least some fear involved.

While the connection between fear and control may be relatively easy to see in most situations, it can be harder to discern the relationship between fear, hope and faith. And even if we understand this relationship, it is sometimes a struggle to maintain our hope and faith when life feels like it has spun out of control. It is easy to be hopeful when things are going well. But what is faith? The world's religious and secular literature is filled with examples of men and women who displayed herculean faith in the face of overwhelming odds. Marcus Borg noted that Christ's freedom from fear was "grounded in the Spirit." Put another way, we might say that the person who can graciously make room in his soul for the uncontrollable aspects of life must somehow be connected with something beyond himself—some kind of meaning system, being, presence or power—that allows him to trust that he will exist and endure in spite of threats to his existence. This is the essence of faith.

As Thomas Aquinas suggested, hope is about things that are not in hand while faith is about things that are not seen. People who have grown up with support and care acquire trust and therefore the hope that life will work out even when it hurts to be alive. But sometimes life becomes so painful, even overwhelming, that hope isn't enough to sustain us. It is at these times that people who believe in something unseen manage better than people who don't. A recent poll by Poloma and Gallup indicated that 20 percent of agnostics and atheists reported praying at least once a day. While this appears to be a contradiction, it makes sense if we are willing to acknowledge the universality of the human need to connect with something beyond ourselves simply because life is bigger than us.

The human brain is wired to experience fear for a reason. Fear gives us the wisdom to avoid danger and to thus endure longer in this life. Without fear we would repeatedly walk into a busy street until we are run over by a speeding car. But the human brain is also wired to experience magic, mystery, wonder and astonishment, which differentiates us from other creatures. This ability to be open to possibilities, to imagine what is not at hand and to believe that there is a reason for our existence, is also part of our physical being. To deny our spirituality is to deny that we are human, and worse, it is ultimately to be burdened with terror and cynicism.

A simple fact of life is that every single human being on earth experiences loss, disappointment and eventually death. Those who are unable to connect with something beyond themselves end up vaguely but pervasively depressed or angry, because they discover that they can't control the universe. Those who have a rigid, immature faith end up bitter and angry, because in their concrete, literal understanding of spirituality, they mistakenly believe that life will always be pleasant if only they "follow the rules" and "do everything right."

LOVE IS ALL AROUND

The recent renewed fascination with angels suggests that as a nation we are hungry for spiritual connectedness. Our world is complicated, and many of us have become disconnected from each other and long for solutions to our loneliness. We need to believe that someone cares, that someone or something out there wants to help us get through this trying life. Spirituality is not so much about what is done to us or for us, as it is about how open we are to what is there, even if we can't always see it. And spirituality includes the ability to be open to the small earthly gifts that flutter in and out of our lives every day. The truly spiritual people whom we admire appear quite ordinary and grounded in their daily existence, and yet they possess a remarkable but unassuming openness to, and reverence for, these small gifts.

A man was having a very difficult year that he described as "the second most stressful year of my life." On the day that all of these stresses came to a head, he found himself rushing around his house, packing for a trip, answering last-minute phone calls, shuffling papers and praying consciously for some relief. He jumped in his car and drove to the gas station to fill his tank, still praying that he would just make it through the day. As he raced home and pulled back into his driveway, he spotted his electrician walking out of the garage. The electrician was a big, friendly man with a strong voice and a realistic view of life.

The man said hello. The electrician said that he had corrected the wiring problem in the garage. The man thanked him. The electrician headed for his truck. The man said he was in a hurry. They knew each other casually. The electrician turned back quickly and asked the man how his business was doing. The man said it was going well, which it was. In his booming voice the electrician yelled, "You do a great job with your business!" as he slammed the door to his truck and drove off to his next job.

The man rushed into his house, his heart racing, to continue packing. He just wanted an end to the stress. He passed his wife in the hall. She was packing, too. He went into the bedroom to get some clothes and then stopped dead in his tracks. His wife rushed by to get her suitcase. He put out his hand and stopped her gently. She smiled, surprised at this gesture of connection amidst their hurriedness. "What?" she asked. His body released the stress as if every cell in him had simultaneously exhaled. He relaxed and said, "I just had to stop for a second. Joe just left. On his way out, he matter-of-factly said I was doing a great job. I almost didn't hear it. I was so rushed I almost didn't hear it. But that one little comment went right to my soul. I've been under so much pressure that I sometimes think I am totally alone and no one appreciates me."

His wife put her arms around him warmly and said, "We all appreciate you very much. You take good care of us. And we need to take better care of you." He felt the knot in his stomach unwind and disappear as he breathed deeply for the first time in days. As they headed down the highway toward their destination, the man wondered what might have happened had he not stopped momentarily to accept the tiny gift that his electrician had given him, and how stressful this day might have been had he not given the gift to his wife who, in turn, gave it back to him. He marveled at how mysterious, surprising and fragile life is, and how grateful he was for the life that he had.

Was the electrician an angel in disguise? Did an angel prod the electrician to turn around and speak to the man just before he got in his truck? Did an angel prompt the man to focus on what the electrician had said? Or was the man simply ready and open to receive the goodness that is always in our midst? Does it matter why?

Good things do come to an end and then other good things are always around to replace them, but only if we are open to the possibility of goodness. And yes, bad things do happen. Los Angeles will have other earthquakes, Kansas will have other tornadoes, Florida will have other hurricanes and Minnesota will probably have another blizzard. The rhythms of life do not go away just because we want them to. But as we pass through this door to adulthood with amazement and anticipation—as we walk into the world of hope, faith and spirituality—we discover that love is all around us and then life is not so frightening.

Part III

Payoffs

Chapter 21

THE PRICES AND THE PAYOFFS OF ADULTHOOD

There is a great price to pay for passing through the doors to adulthood. After all, who really wants to admit that life isn't always fair? Or that we can't and won't get everything our hearts desire? We may have been told, and we may still believe, that this is the land of limitless opportunity, but life is bigger than any of us, and there are clear limits to what each of us can do. But who really wants to face that disappointing fact? Who wants to struggle with the guilt that comes after saying "no" to a close friend or relative? Can't we just keep saying "yes" all the time? Who wants to acknowledge that justice isn't always served? Or that despite our outrage at perceived injustice, we may have a hard enough time just keeping our own houses in order, let alone trying to save the whole world?

When we learn how politics work, we may become disillusioned and feel hopeless. When we discover that our parents aren't gods, or that they aren't demons, we may feel confused. As children we see life as simple, black-and-white, good and bad, clear-cut, one-or-the-other, because that is how the mind of a child perceives things. For an adult who isn't a grown-up yet, the attractive part about this simplistic thinking is that we don't really have to think at all—if you're different than me on some irrelevant dimension like skin color, I can hate you; and if you're similar to me on some irrelevant dimension, I can befriend you even if you're dishonest or manipulative.

Yes, there is a dear price to pay for opening up the doors to adulthood. It is scary at first. It may unleash emotions we thought were permanently sealed behind concrete and steel. As adults, we have to struggle instead of continually trying to return to the safety of the womb. We can't be on center stage all the time. We have to acknowledge our limits. We have to take responsibility for our lives. We have to make choices. We can't blame everyone else for our unhappiness. We can't stamp our little feet angrily and have tantrums in the grocery store whenever someone won't metaphorically "buy us a candy bar at the check-out counter." And after all is said and done, it is just plain sad to say "goodbye" to the innocence and myths of childhood.

Because it is painful to open these doors to adulthood, some of us wait a long time before we do so; and some of us choose not to suffer the hardship at all, and so remain forever locked in a childhood fantasy, never to experience the richness, depth, subtlety, darkness, complexity, magic and wonder of the adult world. To be a child in an adult body is to miss out on the exquisite textures, shadows and edges of life. It is to be blind to the painful, fleeting beauty of bright fall leaves shouting gloriously from every hilltop, because we want summer to last one more day. Bemoaning the advent of winter, we are numb to the magnificent, momentary beauty at hand.

To be a child in an adult body is not to be innocent, it is to be naive, powerless and victimized. When we were young, we may have dreamed of the day when we would be grown up and could do whatever we wanted, whenever we wanted. We didn't realize back then how many responsibilities would be attached to those freedoms about which we fantasized. This is the tradeoff—to remain childishly oblivious to the magnificent incomprehensibility of the universe, or to embrace the paradoxes and eternal unfolding of creation that are there for each of us to behold within our own lifetimes. It is a choice.

Some people fight hard to avoid opening the doors to the soul of adulthood. As they leave middle age, they literally go kicking and screaming into their last decades, fighting with physical decline and the inevitable rhythms of life and death that always prevail. Other people courageously open one door, then another and another. With each opening, they grieve what they leave behind, and they celebrate what will open up before them. They look back at their childhoods to see who they have been, and as they tie up loose ends and spin new threads, they can feel the faint stirrings of wisdom and soulfulness deep inside. Like the man in chapter 1, there is always pain and heartache when we grow. Nobody said it would be easy.

To be an adult means to experience friendship with depth. It means appreciating one's emotional life without being a slave to it. It means having character and wisdom, and the enjoyment that comes with sharing those qualities with the next generation that comes along. It means being connected with all of humanity in a way that is impossible for a child, because it is not within a child's grasp. It means being able to experience love in the way that the great sages of history have described it—without jealousy, envy, fear or competition. Being an adult means to struggle at deeper and deeper layers of soul, but with less and less stress as we mature.

Eventually, adulthood means that we can release enough of our innate narcissism so that we can truly care. In a poignant expression of his own struggle with these issues, Sean Murray wrote:

> I believe our world and the whole of humanity in these days longs for a flood of graciousness, in the form of compassion, to be let loose upon it from whatever source— because we live in times when the "very stones" must be on the verge of crying out, since those who have been entrusted with the task of ministering graciousness are strangely silent.

An adult is not strangely silent. With love, power and graciousness, an adult will accept the inevitable tradeoffs that life offers, but will also continue to struggle, continue to appreciate, continue to hope and believe, and continue to listen to what the universe is saying. With integrity and honor, and with respect for traditions as well as for innovations, an adult will work throughout life to deepen his or her understanding of self, others and the complex bonds that connect each of us to one another and to life itself.

Notes

Our previous books, referred to on occasion in the present work, are as follows:

Friel, J.C., & Friel, L.D. *Adult Children: The Secrets of Dysfunctional Families.* Deerfield Beach, FL: Health Communications, Inc., 1988.

Friel, J.C., & Friel, L.D. *An Adult Child's Guide to What's "Normal."* Deerfield Beach, FL: Health Communications, Inc., 1990.

Friel, J.C. *The Grown-up Man: Heroes, Healing, Honor, Hurt, Hope.* Deerfield Beach, FL: Health Communications, Inc., 1991.

Friel, J.C. *Rescuing Your Spirit.* Deerfield Beach, FL: Health Communications, Inc., 1993.

CHAPTER 1
Life's Delicate Structures

1. Erik Erikson's work is cited throughout this book. His most well-known books are:

Erikson, E.H. *Childhood and Society.* New York: W.W. Norton and Company, 1950.

Erikson, E.H. *Identity: Youth and Crisis.* New York: W.W. Norton and Company, 1968.

2. Jean Piaget's work is also referred to several times and is represented by the following:

Piaget, J. *The Origin of Intelligence in Children.* New York: International Universities Press, 1936.

Piaget, J. *The Psychology of Intelligence.* New York: Harcourt Brace, 1950.

3. Flavell, J.H. *The Developmental Psychology of Jean Piaget.* Princeton, NJ: Van Nostrand Company, Inc., 1963.

4. Jerome Kagan is so prolific that we refer you to any good developmental psychology textbook or to a professional textbook such as:

5. Mussen, P.H. (1970). *Carmichael's Manual of Child Psychology.* New York: John Wiley & Sons, Inc., 1970.

CHAPTER 2
Extremes

The notion of extremes as problematic is so much a part of being human that it has been written about from antiquity until the present, from Aristotle to Aaron Beck and Albert Ellis.

CHAPTER 3
Struggle

1. Sigmund Freud's work can be examined in any good general psychology text, or the reader may wish to read:

Freud, S. *An Outline of Psychoanalysis.* New York: Norton and Company, 1949.

Freud, S. *Civilization and its Discontents.* London: Hogarth Press, 1955.

2. Jung, C. G. *Modern Man in Search of a Soul.* New York: Harcourt, Brace, & World, 1933.

CHAPTER 4
Resistance

1. Koestenbaum, P. *Existential Sexuality: Choosing to Love.* Englewood Cliffs, NJ: Prentice-Hall, 1974.

2. Rilke, Rainer Maria (See page 40).

3. Sykes, C.J. *A Nation of Victims: The Decay of the American Charcater.* New York: St. Martin's Press, 1992.

CHAPTER 5
The Unconscious

1. LaBerge, S. *Lucid Dreaming: The Power of Being Awake and Aware in Your Deams.* New York: Ballantine Books, 1985.

CHAPTER 6
Entitlement

1. Sykes cited previously.

2. Alexis de Tocqueville, *Democracy in America*, Vol. 2, 105-106, was quoted in Sykes' book.

CHAPTER 7
Disappointment

1. Moore, T., *Care of the Soul: A Guide for Cultivating Depth and Sacredness in Everyday Life.* New York: HarperCollins, 1992.

2. Bly, R. *Iron John: A Book About Men.* New York: Addison-Wesley Publishing Co., 1990.

CHAPTER 8
Self-Esteem Myths

The self-esteem movement has some very positive aspects to it, such as respect for children's dignity. But we believe that some teachers, parents and so-called experts on self-esteem have gone to an extreme. There may be other writers who agree with us, but we take full responsibility for the opinions expressed in this chapter, despite whatever criticism we may receive for them.

CHAPTER 9
The Dignity of Loneliness

1. Masterson, J.F. *The Search for the Real Self: Unmasking the Personality Disorders of Our Age.* New York: The Free Press, 1988.

2. Charad, P. Personal communication, 1994.

CHAPTER 10
Trade-Offs

1. Erikson cited previously.

2. Peck, R.C. *Psychological Developments in the Second Half of Life.* In B.L. Neugarten (Ed.) *Middle Age and Aging.* Chicago: University of Chicago Press, 1968.

CHAPTER 11
Narcissism

1. Lasch, C. *The Culture of Narcissism: American Life in an Age of Diminishing Expectations.* New York: W.W. Norton and Company, Inc., 1991.

2. Moore's and Masterson's books cited previously.

3. *Diagnostic and Statistical Manual of Mental Disorders, Fourth Edition (DSM-IV).* American Psychiatric Association, 1994.

4. Elkind, D. "Egocentrism in Adolescence." *Child Development,* 38 (1967), 1025-1034.

5. Erikson cited previously.

6. Holtzermann, J. Personal communication, 1994.

CHAPTER 12
Victimhood

1. Sykes cited previously.

2. St. Paul psychologists James Maddock and Noel Larson are two of the nation's leading experts on treating victims and perpetrators. Their new clinical textbooks are:

Understanding and Treating Family Sexual Abuse: An Ecological Approach, W.W. Norton and Company, 1995.

Treating Victims and Perpetrators of Sexual Abuse: An Ecological Approach, W.W. Norton and Company, 1995.

CHAPTER 13
Beyond Dysfunctional Roles

1. Rogers, C. *Becoming Partners: Marriage and Its Alternatives.* New York: Delta Books, 1973.

2. Satir, V. *Conjoint Family Therapy.* Palo Alto, CA: Science and Behavior Books, 1967.

3. Maslow, A.H. *Motivation and Personality.* New York: Harper and Brothers, 1974.

4. Wegscheider, S. *Another Chance: Hope and Help for the Alcoholic Family.* Palo Alto, CA: Science and Behavior Books, 1981.

CHAPTER 14
Victim to Adult

1. Naas, D. Personal communication, 1994.

2. Hale, E.E.

CHAPTER 15
Love, Power and Graciousness

1. We have carried around this quote from Holmes for over a decade but have been unable to find the exact reference. We would appreciate any reader's help in enlightening us about its origin.

2. Likewise for the quote from Erikson.

3. Milton, J. *Paradise Lost.* Edited by Scott Elledge. New York: W.W. Norton, 1975.

4. Johnson, S. From Boswell, *Journal of a Tour to the Hebrides* (1785), August 20, 1773.

CHAPTER 16
Releasing

1. The quote from Ecclesiastes is from the King James Version, 1973.

CHAPTER 17
Appreciation

We would especially like to thank Sean and Kate Murray of Cahir, County Tipperary, for their gracious hospitality and depth of vision that they shared with us while we were in Ireland.

CHAPTER 18
Integrity, Honor and Accountability

1. Bennett, W. *The Book of Virtues: A Treasury of the World's Great Moral Stories.* New York: Simon & Schuster Trade, 1993.

2. See previous note for references to Piaget's work.

3.. Brennan, L. Personal communication, 1994.

CHAPTER 19
Tradition, Structure and Discipline

We are aware that England has its own unique problems and that having a royal family can be as painful and dysfunctional at times as not having one. We are also sadly aware that for the first time, automatic weapons have been introduced into London in association with drug-related crime.

CHAPTER 20
Faith, Hope and Spirituality

1. Urie Bronfenbrenner's conclusion was reported in an old issue of *Psychology Today* in the late 1960s or early 1970s.

2. Borg, M.J. *Jesus: A New Vision.* San Francisco: Harper & Row, 1987.

3. Theroux, P. *Translating LA: A Tour of the Rainbow City.* New York: W.W. Norton and Company, 1994.

4. Statistics from Poloma and Gallup cited in *Newsweek*, January 6, 1992, in an article entitled "T*alking To God: An Intimate Look At The Way We Pray.*"

CHAPTER 21
The Prices and the Payoffs of Adulthood

1. Murray, S. *God's Graciousness—Implications for Church and Ministry.* Cahir, County Tipperary, Ireland.

About the Authors

John Friel and Linda Friel are psychologists in private practice in St. Paul, Minnesota and are known throughout the U.S., Canada, England and Ireland for their therapeutic and training expertise in the areas of family systems, survivors of unhealthy childhoods, depression, anxiety, addictions and personality disorders. They are the founders and national directors of the ClearLife/Lifeworks Clinic, which is a special four-day therapy program to help people move beyond the painful patterns of childhood shortages. Their first two books, *Adult Children: The Secrets Of Dysfunctional Families* and *An Adult Child's Guide To What's "Normal"* are now considered to be classics in the field and are widely read by both professionals and the general public.

They offer individual, couples and family therapy as well as conducting several weekly, ongoing men's and women's therapy groups. In addiction, John Friel maintains an active training and speaking schedule, and is known for his practical, innovative, powerful and compassionate presentation and training style. Whether speaking to the general public or just to professionals, he has the ability to handle difficult or painful material with a fine balance of competence, sensitivity, gentle humor and professionalism that has made him on of the top trainers in the county.

Linda and John have three wonderful, full-grown children who are out of the nest, a calm, soulful yellow

Labrador Retriever, and a 20-pound Cockapoo with a magical spirit. They contemplate increasing their canine population, but their children already wink and tell them that they've gone to the dogs.

They can be reached at:

Linda D. Friel, M.A.
John C. Friel, Ph.D.
Friel Associates/ClearLife
Shoreview, MN 55126
612•482-7982
Fax•486-8906